Foundation of Freshman English Writing

Christopher R. Sanders

Table of Contents

Acknowledgements

Writer: Chris Sanders

Writing Supervisor: Sun Chang

Editors: Dean V. Beckman
Mata Rakanui
Gwen Atkinson
Margaret McElhenny

Editing Supervisor: Sun Chang

Bibliography

Davies, Dawn; MacMartin, Fiona; MacRae, Susan; Brown, Lucien. (2001) Campus Connections II, Soongsil University

SETI, (2010.12.01) http://en.wikipedia.org/wiki/SETI

Coco Chanel, (2010.11.24) http://en.wikipedia.org/wiki/Coco_Chanel

Eakins, Lara. Transition Words, (2010.10.15) http://larae.net/write/transition.html

Russell, Tony; Brizee, Allen; Angeli, Elizabeth. MLA Formatting and Style Guide (2010.11.10) http://owl.english.purdue.edu/owl/resource/747/01/

McKenna, Kelly. (2010) Bear Necessity: Korea (http://bearnecessitykorea.com/)

Hello Kitty, (2010.12.13) http://en.wikipedia.org/wiki/Hello_Kitty

The Battle of Antietam (2010.07.23) http://en.wikipedia.org/wiki/Battle_of_Antietam

All About Vodka (2010.08.14) http://www.tastings.com/spirits/vodka.html

How to Say Cheers/Slainte in Different Countries (2010.08.14) http://www.awa.dk/glosary/slainte.htm

Jaffe-Gill, Ellen, M.A.; Kemp, Gina, M.A.; Robinson, Lawrence. (2010.11) Improving Your Memory (2010.09.07) http://helpguide.org/life/improving_memory.htm

Safety Belt Statistics (2010.08.08) http://www.jmu.edu/safetyplan/vehicle/generaldriver/safetybelt.shtml

TED (conference) (2010.08.14) http://en.wikipedia.org/wiki/TED_(conference)

Korea university tuition sees five-year surge (Feb 20, 2010) Asia One Education http://www.asiaone.com/News/Education/Story/A1Story20100220-199862.html

Spring Semester

Foundation of Freshman English Writing

Unit 01 What Are Paragraphs?

Objectives

- What are paragraphs?
- The 6 rules of paragraphs
- Titles for writing

What Are Paragraphs?

This is not a paragraph.
Writing can be challenging but fun.
There is no indent.
Instead of following each other, the sentences start on new lines.
some of the sentences have grammar mistakes. Or no verbs.
Furthermore, some of the sentences are not related to the main idea.
If you see these problems, then it is not a proper paragraph.

This is a paragraph. You'll notice that the first word starts several spaces to the right. That is called an indent. The sentences follow each other on the same line instead of starting on new lines. Also, all the sentences are about the same topic, and they are all grammatically proper. When you see a group of sentences like this, you are looking at a paragraph.

You have probably seen many, many paragraphs since you started studying English. They are used to separate several sentences about one idea from sentences about another idea. Without paragraphs, we would have a difficult time understanding what we are reading; everything would blur together. If you read books or essays from the 1700 and 1800's, you will find few paragraphs. At that time, authors rarely separated their sentences from each other, so it is very challenging to understand their work in some cases (their sentences were also very long, sometimes several pages long).

To make a good paragraph, follow these six rules.

The 6 Rules of Paragraphs

1) **The first sentence is indented.**
The first word of the first sentence starts about 5 spaces to the right.

2) **The first letter and proper names are capitalized.**
The first letter of the first word of a sentence; the first letter of all names(people, places, book and movie titles); most abbreviations (DVD, UN, USA); the first letter of days, months and holidays; and I meaning me are all capitalized.

3) **Every sentence ends in punctuation (. ! ?).**

4) **Each sentence has a subject and a** predicate, or main, verb, **and they match each other in voice and number (subject-verb agreement).**

5) **All sentences are about one main idea.**
A paragraph can only be about one idea and every sentence must support this idea.

6) **Sentences do not start on new lines.**
When one sentence ends, the next sentence starts two spaces to the right of the period (or question mark, exclamation point). Do not begin the next sentence on a new line. This is called block style.

Rule #1 The first sentence is indented.

The main purpose of a paragraph is to separate ideas. The main way to do this is to indent. An indent is a small empty space at the beginning of the first line. On paper, this is about 5 to 7 letters long, or about two fingers wide. When typing in a computer program like Microsoft Word or Hangul, hitting the Tab key will create the indent for you. On the Internet, you can't use the Tab key to make an indent. In these situations, you should make a full line break so that the second paragraph is clearly separated from the first.

The Indent

The people of Bali have only four names. The first child born is named Wayan. ....

Rule #2 The first letter and proper names are capitalized.

One of the fundamental rules of English writing is to use proper capitalization. There are many specific things that are capitalized, but the main ones to remember are:

- The first letter of a sentence
- The names of people (Kim Yuna, Sherlock Holmes, Madonna) and places (Australia, Gangnam, E-Mart)
- Abbreviations (television -> TV, random access memory -> RAM)
- Days, months, and holidays (Tuesday, April, Chuseok)
- The word I meaning 'me'.

Rule #3 Every sentence ends in punctuation.

Another fundamental writing rule: always put a period, question mark, or exclamation point at the end of every sentence.

. ? !

Rule #4 Each sentence has a subject and a main verb.

By definition, a sentence is a subject and a verb together. If one of these is missing, it isn't a sentence. The verb needs to match the case of the subject as well. That means if the subject is a singular third person noun, the verb usually needs to have a "s" at the end.

I walk home every day.
You walk home every day.
Sarah walks home every day.
Wonho walks home every day.
The robot walks home every day.

We walk home every day.
You walk home every day.
Sarah and Dami walk home every day.
Wonho and David walk home every day.
The robot and the chicken walk home every day.

Rule #5 Every paragraph is about one main idea.

As we noted earlier, the purpose of a paragraph is to separate ideas. Therefore, each paragraph should be about one idea only. Anything that is not related to that idea – which is expressed by the topic sentence – should be removed or changed to fit. Furthermore, the sentences in the paragraph should all be the same style. If you are talking about something scientific and using the third person (no "you" or "I"), then having one sentence that is casual and says "you" wouldn't fit.

Hello Emotions

If I say "picture Hello Kitty in your mind", I'm sure you will see the famous white cartoon cat with the bow on her ear. Did you see a mouth? Probably not; since her creation in 1975, she has never had a mouth. A ~~cat's mouth usually looks like a ship's anchor.~~ Why doesn't Hello Kitty have a mouth? What do you feel when you see her? If you are like most people, you probably think that she is feeling like you are feeling. If you are sad, then Hello Kitty looks sad ~~too. Sadness is a normal human emotion but long-term sadness can cause health problems~~. If you are happy, her blank face looks happy to you too. That may be part of Hello Kitty's popularity.

Rule #6 Sentences do not start on new lines.

A paragraph keeps all its sentences together. The next sentence starts a space or two after the period (or question mark or exclamation point) of the sentence before it.

Drinking mate is an important cultural activity in Paraguay, Argentina and southern Brazil. The tea is drunk through a metal straw from a large cup, which is passed from person to person.

People in this part of South America believe that mate helps to relax the mind and keep the body cool.

Furthermore, because mate is ⋯

Drinking mate is an important cultural activity in Paraguay, Argentina and southern Brazil. The tea is drunk through a metal straw from a large cup, which is passed from person to person. People in this part of South America believe that mate helps to relax the mind and keep the body cool. Furthermore, because mate is ⋯

Exercises

Exercise 1.1

Underline the subject and the main (predicate) verb in each sentence.

1) On Wednesday, Dami and Wonhee ate some Italian food.
2) The cat watched us as we sat in the park.
3) Did you see the movie?
4) Cecilia is my sister.
5) The computer crashes every time I open this program.
6) In my opinion, Winnie the Pooh is the best children's story.
7) Yesterday was Tuesday, wasn't it?
8) According to the news, it might rain tomorrow.
9) Jincheol's skiing trip will be delayed until next week.
10) When he was young, he lived in the Philippines.

Exercise 1.2

Put these sentences in the correct order and make them into a proper paragraph. One sentence doesn't belong.

After the war, he started a business in the new field of computer programming and though he did not become rich, he was able to give a good life to his children.
For me, it's my grandfather.
Pearl Harbor was an important Navy base in Hawaii.
He is the bravest and smartest person I know.
I hope I can follow in his footsteps.
Who is your hero?
He left a farm in a rural Kansas to join the US Army after the Japanese attacked Pearl Harbor.
He won several medals for his brave actions.

Exercise 1.3

Fill in the missing words.

proper	grammar	capitalized	punctuation	subject	six
main idea	blank	follow	rules	right	indented

There are ______ rules or guidelines for writing ______ paragraphs. The first sentence should be ______ several spaces to the ______. If you are typing on a website, though, you can use a ______ line. Secondly, all the sentences should follow proper ______ rules. This means that the first word and proper names should be ______, ending ______ must be used, the ______ and predicate verb must agree with each other, and there should be no fragments or run-on sentences. Next, a paragraph has only one ______ and every sentence should support that idea. If you want to talk about a different topic, you should start a new paragraph. Finally, make sure all the sentences ______ each other; do not put each sentence on its own line. That's a poem, not a paragraph! If you pay attention to these ______, you will be writing good paragraphs in no time.

Exercises

Exercise 1.4

Rewrite the sentences with the proper capitalization.

1. this is my cousin robert from sydney.

2. on monday, october twentieth we're going to see les miserables.

3. luxury products like, prada and gucci, from america and europe can be very expensive in korea.

4. wonbin was having problems with microsoft word, so he didn't finish professor kim's homework assignment.

5. manchester united beat chelsea two goals to one in the game on friday.

6. next wednesday, i am going to busan by ktx.

7. when i saw haesun on christmas day, She said her Father was in the Hospital.

8. if you want to go to harvard university, you'll have to speak english really well.

9. after the end of the vietnam war, the vietnamese government changed the name of saigon to ho chi min city.

10. as the h.m.s. titanic was sinking in the atlantic ocean, the crew sent out an s.o.s. signal.

Exercise 1.5

Add the proper ending punctuation to each sentence.

1. Do you know what time the movie starts ____
2. Oh no ____ There's a fire in the kitchen ____
3. The library is closed on Sunday ____
4. You want to get some coffee with me ____
5. Americans celebrate their Independence Day on July 4th ____
6. Help ____ Call the police ____
7. Is Alex from Canada or England ____
8. Stop right there ____
9. We bought a new TV last week ____
10. Can you hand me a pen, please ____

Exercise 1.6

Fix the problems with the verbs in the following sentences.

1. Chang see a new movie every week
2. They always eats at restaurants, never at home.
3. Yale are a major university in the United States.
4. A simple notebook computer cost about $600.
5. Keith like Mary, so he are asking her for a date this weekend.
6. There is many problems with this design.
7. The professor and her students is in the computer lab.
8. I are going to the cafeteria, do you want to come?
9. We gets lots of rain during the monsoon.
10. Korea have four distinct seasons.

Exercises

Exercise 1.7

Are these actually sentences? Mark X if it does not have a subject or main verb.

1. __We to the park every Sunday.
2. __Even if we do.
3. __Alexis asked Tony for some money.
4. __Comes every day at 3:30pm and buys a newspaper.
5. __Because Jaemin can't eat spicy food.
6. __Lotus flowers are a common symbol in Buddhist art.
7. __The train station farthest from our house, on the Bundang line.
8. __Since no one here smokes anymore.
9. __So in the end we decided to eat pizza.
10. __The color red always my favorite color since I was a child.

Exercise 1.8

Rewrite these sentences into a proper paragraph. Don't forget the indent, and remember that sentences do not start on new lines.

Different cultures have different ideas about time.
In some countries, it is very important to be on time.
Being late will make people angry.
People in these countries like to do one task, complete it, and the move to the next.
In other countries, however, people are more relaxed about time.
Being late is not a problem.
People often have different appointments at the same time and do many different activities together.

Unit 02 | Parts of a Paragraph

Objectives

- Examine two styles: descriptive and persuasive
- Learn the parts of paragraphs
- Understand the main idea
- Review the difference between fact and opinion

Types of Paragraphs

There are many kinds of paragraphs: descriptive, persuasive, instructional, narrative, exposition, and so forth. In this course, we will focus on two of the most common, the descriptive paragraph and the persuasive.

The Descriptive Paragraph

This kind of paragraph tells the reader some information; in other words it describes something to the reader. It could tell the reader about a new movie, the author's first boyfriend or girlfriend, the life of Albert Einstein, or the reason why newly married couples often go to Jeju Island.

My First Love: Coffee

I am not a morning person. If I have to do something in the morning, I must have a cup of coffee. Not only does it give me energy, but it makes me feel warm and happy. The rich smell of the roasted beans always brings a smile to my face. The sharp, slightly bitter taste of a good Columbian or Kenyan blend dances on my tongue and shocks my body awake. Even if I never marry, I will always have coffee in my life.

The Persuasive Paragraph

The purpose of a persuasive paragraph is to express the author's opinion and change the way other people think or act. These kinds of paragraphs are used for many reasons, from politics to advertising and everything in between.

Privacy at Risk

Do you use social networks like Facebook, Cyworld, or Twitter? If you do, you must be careful about your privacy. It can be very fun to share photos, post comments about what you are doing, and 'check-in' at places with Foursquare or Facebook Places. But if you do, you could be putting yourself at risk. No matter what settings you choose, it is always possible that someone you don't know can see your online activities. People's homes have been robbed when they posted online that they were going on vacation. Stalkers can use social networks to follow their obsession. No one is saying that people shouldn't use social networks. Just use them responsibly and never share anything you don't want the world to know. You never know who's following you online.

Parts of a Paragraph

A paragraph is made up of 3 parts: the introduction, the body, and the conclusion. The introduction gets the reader interested in the subject and tells the reader the main idea of the paragraph. The body explains the issue or offers arguments to support the author's opinion. Finally, the conclusion usually summarizes the main points and offers some sort of closing statement. Of course, in many cases, you will also add a title to your paragraph.

Privacy at Risk — Title

Introduction

Do you use social networks like Facebook, Cyworld, or Twitter? If you do, you must be careful about your privacy. It can be very fun to share photos, post comments about what you are doing, and 'check-in' at places with Foursquare or Facebook Places. But if you do, you could be putting yourself at risk. No matter what settings you choose, it is always possible that someone you don't know can see your online activities. People's homes have been robbed when they posted online that they were going on vacation. Stalkers can use social networks to follow their obsession. No one is saying that people shouldn't use social networks. Just use them responsibly and never share anything you don't want the world to know. You never know who's following you online.

Opening statement

Topic sentence

Body

Conclusion

Summary

Closing statement

Fact Versus Opinion

Facts are true information. Opinions are people's ideas or feelings about things. A fact would be "It is 3 o'clock." An opinion would be "It's the best time of day!" Probably everyone would agree that the time is 3 o'clock. Most people would not think that 3 is the best time of the day.

It's important to understand what kind of material to put into the body of your paragraph. In descriptive paragraphs, you will usually give factual information: who, what, where, when, why, how. But also, descriptive paragraphs often include sensory information: how things smell, sound, feel, taste, look. These will be a mix of fact and opinion. When writing a descriptive paragraph, you'll want to share some facts about the topic, but also some of your feelings about it too.

In a persuasive essay, you are trying to change people's minds or actions with your opinion. So, in the body, you need to use evidence to support your opinion. Data, statistics, quotes, information from books and articles, and examples will usually help people accept your opinion more easily than if it is just your own idea.

Exercise 2.1

Read the following topic sentences. Do you think they are for descriptive or persuasive paragraphs? Write D or P next to each sentence.

1) There are many delicious foods in Korean cuisine.
2) I believe that students should do volunteer work in order to graduate.
3) I learned many valuable lessons from my grandparents.
4) The city must do more to solve the traffic problem.
5) In my opinion, studying abroad is the only way to succeed in the global business environment.
6) Paris has several stunning museums worth visiting.
7) Raising a pet can teach children valuable life skills.
8) Children should raise pets to learn valuable life skills.
9) Coco Chanel was one of the most influential fashion designers in history.
10) Several factors are responsible for the global economic crisis.

Exercise 2.2

Read the following paragraphs. Which one is persuasive? Which one is descriptive?

1. Descriptive / Persuasive

My granddaughter is six years old. She loves to play with her friends and draw pictures. But, she does not have much time to do these fun things because she goes to an English kindergarten at 9am every day. After she returns home at 3pm, she meets a Korean tutor for an hour, and then she goes with her brother to tae-kwon-do class. Why do our children have to study so much? When do they have time to be children? By the time they reach university, they are tired of studying. Our children cannot and should not endure so much stress. We MUST look at ways to change the education system so that children have a chance to be children.

2. Descriptive / Persuasive

September 17th, 1862 was the single bloodiest day in United States history. On that day, near the town of Sharpsburg along Antietam Creek 23,000 men died fighting in the American Civil War. The leader of the Southern Army, General

Exercises

Robert E. Lee had begun an invasion of the Northern States as part of the Maryland Campaign. The Northern leader, Major General Geore McClellan, had many more troops than Lee, but due to poor strategy failed to defeat the Southern army. In that day of the Battle of Antietam, more Americans were killed than in any other battle in the nation's history.

Exercise 2.3

Underline the topic sentence and conclusion in each of these paragraphs.

1) Toys were so much better when I was a child. First of all, we had Transformers! These are the pinnacle of toy goodness. They looked like cars or trucks or planes, but with some twisting and popping, you had a cool robot. And there was a cartoon that featured them, too. There were also Lego blocks. Sure there is Lego today, but the ones we had when I was a kid were astounding. Hundreds of different space craft were waiting to be created. You could get a small box that built a simple Lunar Rover or a huge box with hundreds of pieces to construct entire space colonies! Hours and hours of joy and creativity were waiting inside the box. Children today just don't have the great toys I did.

2) Web page functionality has improved dramatically since the Internet was created. In the early 1990's, web pages were simply text and a few pictures. Users were limited to very slow connections by the phone wires and technology of the day, so web pages could not deliver large media files. As broadband technology became more and more common, various functionalities were added to web pages. Videos could be watched directly from a web site, interactive games written in Java or Flash became common, and users could create larger and more interactive sites. As connection speeds increase, web pages will only become more exciting.

Exercise 2.4

Write a topic sentence for each of the paragraphs below.

1. ______________________________ First, we have to use the proper trash bags and put our recycling in the proper containers. If your building doesn't have a recycling bin, get together with your neighbors to buy one; they aren't expensive. Furthermore, we mustn't litter! If you see litter on the ground, why don't you pick it up and throw it away? Take down old posters and ads on walls and streetlights, too. Finally, when you have some free time, tend the grass and trees around your home. So, instead of complaining about how dirty your neighborhood is, do something about it!

2. ______________________________ The first thing to consider is the processor's speed. You'll want to use your laptop for as long as possible, so if you buy a fast processor now, the laptop will keep up with new software longer. Second, consider the screen's size. The larger the screen, the more expensive the laptop is. Will you be happy with a 15 inch screen, or do you need the whole 17 inches? The next issue is weight. If you think you'll carry your laptop around often, you'll need a lighter computer. Finally, check out the warranty. Make sure it covers all the problems you may face. If you keep these in mind, you will be happy with your new laptop.

3. ______________________________ The most important lesson I learned from Mittens' death was that everything comes to an end. It was a hard lesson for a 7 year old kid to learn, but when my beloved pet cat died, I had to grow up a little bit just to understand it. Of course my parents tried to comfort me, buying me toys and giving me ice cream, but I didn't want to be cheered up; I wanted to be sad about Mittens. Eventually, of course, I was able to be happy again, but I have never forgotten my pet, and I never will.

Exercise 2.5

Read each of the topic sentences and statements. Are they facts or opinions? Write F in the box if it is a fact; write O for opinion statements.

President Bush was first elected in 2000.	Korean tradition advises people to eat dog meat in the summer.	Last night's basketball game was horrible!	President Bush is the worst leader in US history.	Sales of books have been increasing every year.	Tony and Susan are the nicest people in the world.
Japan is an evil country.	English education is a multi-billion dollar industry worldwide.	The LA Lakers won the game with 107 points.	I think people should not eat dog meat.	The temperature today will reach 21℃ and the sky will be sunny.	Tony and Susan donate lots of time and money to charity every year.
Pizza is better than hamburgers.	It's clear that we need more English education.	According to a survey, dinner-and-movie dates are still very popular.	Many Koreans have a negative view of Japan.	This weather is beautiful!	Few students study literature these days.
Homosexuality is immoral	Clearly, Chinese goods are dangerous and should not be sold here.	Everyone hates that movie, it's so dumb.	Many Christians are against the idea of gay marriage.	Last year, many Chinese goods had toxic lead and were destroyed.	The movie did not do well in the theaters and many critics gave it bad reviews.

Memo

Unit 03 | The Foundation: Sentence Structure

Objectives

- Review sentence structure
- Learn to avoid common mistakes

Sentence Structure

The foundation of every paragraph is the sentence. As you saw in the 6 Rules of Paragraphs, every sentence must have a subject and a main verb.

Lina studies English at an academy.

subject main verb

In many cases, a sentence also has an object. Adjectives can change the nouns in the sentence to give them more specific meaning.

Lina studies English at an academy.

subject main verb object

Lina studies academic English at an academy.

subject main verb adjective object

Lina studies English diligently.

adverb

Lina studies English quite diligently.

adverb

Clauses

A basic sentence has a subject, a main verb and perhaps an object. But, as sentences get more complicated, you will need to add various kinds of clauses to them.

Examples

The movie that we saw last week was boring.

Because of the floods, the price of vegetables rose more than expected.

The students laughed when the teacher started singing.

On their anniversary, she wanted to eat where they'd met the first time.

According to the secretary in the office, the professor whose classroom is on the third floor had a traffic accident when it snowed.

Sentence Fragments

One problem with clauses is that many people try to use them alone, without a sentence. A clause must be inside of a regular sentence. Be especially careful when using because and since, as well as when, where and who.

✗ Because it was raining

✓ We couldn't go to the park because it was raining.

✗ When you have time.

✓ When you have time, please give me a call.

✗ Speaking of the library.

✓ Speaking of the library, I think the university should build a bigger one.

✗ Since I was young.

✓ I wanted to be a fashion designer since I was young.

Commas

Commas are one of the most problematic pieces of punctuation in English. People are often very confused about how to use them. Look at the list below for comma examples.

Let's eat, Grandpa.
Let's eat Grandpa.
The first sentence is an invitation to your grandfather to have dinner together.
The second sentence is a suggestion for some zombies to turn your grandfather into food!

versus

Guidelines for commas

Lists

Use a comma to separate items in a list.
Please bring a pen, a notebook, the textbook, and your homework to class everyday.

Clauses

Introductory information about the action in the sentence, the reason for why something happened, or other things the reader should know about the sentence are usually separated with a comma.
Since he got a bad grade on the test, Thomas has been studying really hard.
Even if it rains tomorrow, we will have the soccer match.

Extra information

If we want to give the reader some information that doesn't change the meaning of the sentence, we need to uses commas to separate it.
The cat, which Henry loves, caught a mouse.

"which Henry loves" doesn't change the meaning of the sentence "The cat caught a mouse."

My aunt, Elizabeth, lives in Melbourne.

The fact that my aunt's name is Elizabeth doesn't matter If I have only one aunt. If I have two or more aunts, the information is important and should not use commas

My aunt Elizabeth lives in Melbourne. My aunt Caroline moved to Los Angeles last year.

Adjectives

When using several adjectives in a row that are not directly connected to each other, use a comma.

That expensive, new restaurant is not very good.

Quotes

If you are quoting someone, use a comma.

Gandhi once said, "An eye for an eye only ends up making the whole world blind."

Dates, names, locations

Thursday, October 7th, 2010

Christmas Day, 1998

Jefferson, Thomas (Only in an index, encyclopedia, or citation!)

Brooklyn, New York City, New York, United States of America

Sangdo-dong, Dongjak-gu, Seoul, South Korea

Exercises

Exercise 3.1

Look at the pictures. Then make a question and an answer about what the person regularly does. Pay attention to subject/verb agreement. Practice asking and answering each one with a partner.

The first one is done for you.

Question	Action	Answer
Won-seob, Saturday What does Won-seob do on Saturdays?		He plays basketball on Saturdays.
Jamie, Kevin, and Mark, weekend		
diligent student, every week		
Mina, all the time		
Daniel, Wednesday		
Students, every day		

Exercise 3.2

Add an appropriate verb to each sentence. Make sure it follows subject-verb agreement rules.

Examples

Sarah/bibimbap/every day
Sarah eats bibimbap every day.

1. Jinhee/English/two hours a day

2. Claire and Tony/movies/on the weekend

3. The cat/in the sun/every afternoon

4. The teacher/for class/in the evening

5. Ghosts/in the old house

6. On Saturday/I/usually/the park

7. According to this article/black and white/fashionable/this year

8. Prof. Nam/email/everyday

9. At Christmas time/Americans/lots of gifts/for family and friends

10. Johnny Depp's new movie/not/very interesting

Exercises

Exercise 3.3

Correct the mistakes in the following sentences.

0. A cat sit on the mat. sat ____________________

1. Some students was late. ________
2. The answer are wrong. ________
3. A mother and her baby was crossing the street. ________
4. Money and information is important in the global economy. ________
5. Tae-sub don't do his homework. ________
6. Alicia and Ji-yeon wasn't at the meeting. ________
7. Tomorrow the weather are going to be awful. ________
8. If you drinks too much soju, you will be sick tomorrow. ________
9. The new teacher want to learn all the students' names. ________
10. There are a table and lamp in the bedroom. ________

Exercise 3.4

Unscramble the sentences. Add the proper punctuation(. , ?) as needed.

0. to I I go Paris could wish
   I wish I could go to Paris.

1. the landed flower butterfly A on

   ____

2. a teacher of homework gave The lot

   ____

3. bus Stephanie her missed

   ____

4. hand the please me Can book you

   ____

5. some you tired If drink are coffee

   ____

Exercise 3.5

Put a comma in the proper place.

1. On Sunday my family usually goes to church.
2. We're going to need clothes a sleeping bag food and water for the camping trip.
3. Hey Jeongmin did you hear that the test is cancelled?
4. My new address is 415 Maple Street Peoria Illinois 61064.
5. "Let's go" said Sarah to her friends.
6. Last Friday Julie met Michael Henry Sarah and Katie at the Hyatt Hotel.
7. Professor Steven Jones married Doctor Izumi Saito in Vancouver British Columbia Canada on August 15th 2007.
8. I was studying for Prof. Choi's long difficult Chinese exam when my mother Veronica called to tell me to stop by E-mart and buy cheese cereal lettuce and onions.
9. So if Margaret flies to K.L. Malaysia she can save almost 300000 won.
10. On Monday July 23rd Dahyeon prepared an American-style barbecue with sausages hamburgers hot dogs and potato salad.

Unit 04 The Ties That Bind: Unity and Transition

Objectives

- Learn signal and transition words
- See the importance of unity in a paragraph
- Understand what goes into the body of a paragraph

Signal and Transition Words

One of the ways we help our readers understand whatever we are writing about through the use of transition words. Signal or transition words show the relationship of one idea or sentence with the other sentences around it. Using these kinds of words makes it much easier for the reader to understand the main idea.

Continuation, additional information

and	also	another again	and finally	
first of all	furthermore	in addition	last of all	moreover
likewise more	moreover	next	one reason	
other	secondly	similarly	too	with

Contrast, negation

although	but	conversely	despite
different from	even though	however	in contrast
instead of	in spite of	nevertheless	otherwise
the opposite	on the contrary	on the other hand	
rather	still	yet	while
though			

Sequence

first, second, third	A, B, C	since	then	for one thing
next	before now	after	while	in the first place
into (far into the night)	until	last	during	
always	on time	later	earlier	

Illustration

for example	specifically	for instance	to illustrate	such as
much like	in the same way as		similar to	like

Emphasis

most of all	a primary concern	most noteworthy
more than anything else		a major event
pay particular attention to		remember that
a central issue		should be noted
above all		especially important
the basic concept		especially relevant
important to note		the principal item

Cause, condition, or result signals

because if	of	for	from	due to
so	while	then	but	that
until	since	as	whether	in order that
so that	therefore	unless	yet	thus
resulting from	consequently			

Spatial, "where"

between	on	by	here	there
left	right	these	close to	near
this	side	middle	west	beside
east	about	north	south	around
over	under	away	in front of	across
into	behind	toward	beyond	above
below	opposite	upon	outside	upon
outside	inside	over	out	far
in	adjacent	near	next to	

Conclusion

as a result	consequently	finally	from this we see
last of all	in summary	hence	in conclusion
therefore			

Look at the use of signal words in this paragraph.

Better Memory

Quick! Can you remember the 5th digit of pi? When is your aunt's birthday? What colors are on the Indian flag? If you can't remember these things, you want to improve your memory. There are many things you can do to increase your memory power. First, practice 'neurobic' exercises, like taking a shower and dressing with your eyes closed. Second, break your routine. Contrary to what many people think, it's better to study in different places each day so your brain doesn't get too familiar with one place. Furthermore, studying in a new place makes the brain more active as it learns about the place, and this extra activity encourages memorization. Finally, experts suggest using as many senses as possible. According to research, memories associated with smells are the strongest. Therefore, if you want to improve your memory, practice, change your routine, and focus on sensory details. Now all you have to do is remember these steps.

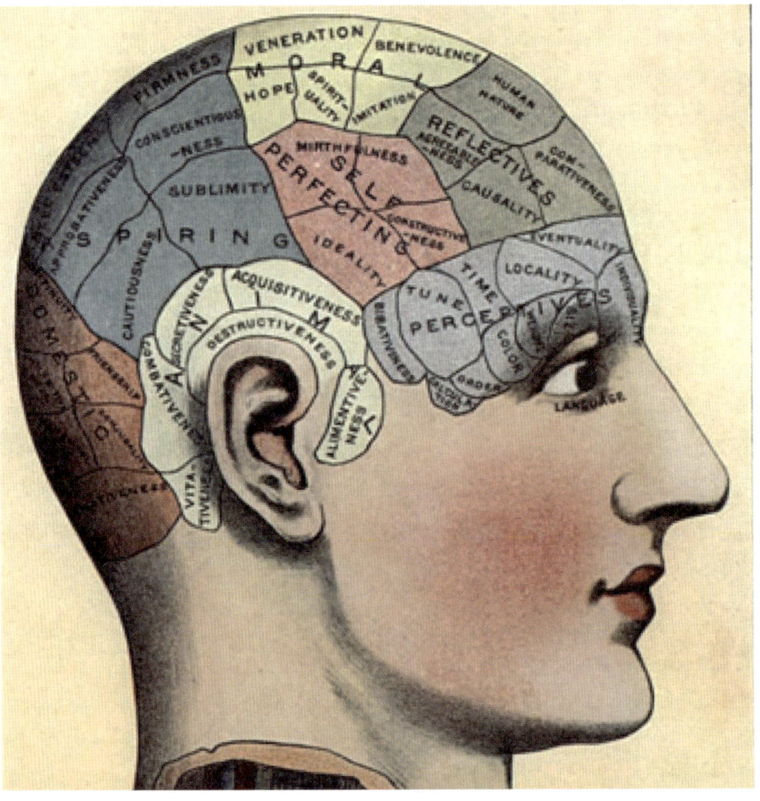

Exercise 4.1

Read the paragraphs below Cross out any sentences that do not belong.

A

Fair Trade Coffee

Do you like coffee? I do. I drink coffee every day. But recently I learned that many coffee shops buy their beans from large companies that do not support their workers well. In fact, many of these companies keep their costs low by using children to do the hardest work. Children should be in school. That's why I now only buy fair trade coffee. Fair trade coffee comes directly from the coffee farmers; no large companies earn money from the farmers' work. Farming is very difficult work for them. Next time you want a cup of joe, please order fair trade coffee. It's the right thing to do.

B

Coco Chanel

If you walk down the street in Gangnam or Apgujeong, you will see many women, and some men, wearing clothes with a double C logo, the emblem for the famous luxury brand Chanel. But do you know who founded this iconic company? Chanel was created by French fashion designer Coco Chanel. She was born Gabreille Chanel in Saumur, France in 1883. Gabreille was a common girl's name. She learned how to make clothes when she was an orphan at age twelve. At 18, she left the orphanage and became a cabaret singer, using the name Coco. She soon fell in love with a rich textile factory owner and started making clothes in her own shops. From there, she became one of the most respected and influential fashion designers in the world. Her life is inspiring to many, rising from a poor orphan to the highest ranks of a glamorous industry. The clothing is very high quality.

Exercises

Exercise 4.2

For the two paragraphs above, fill in the information below.

Paragraph A.

Topic sentence: ______________________________

Supporting detail 1: ______________________________

Supporting detail 2: ______________________________

Supporting detail 3: ______________________________

Paragraph B.

Topic sentence: ______________________________

Supporting detail 1: ______________________________

Supporting detail 2: ______________________________

Supporting detail 3: ______________________________

Supporting detail 4: ______________________________

Exercise 4.3

Read the paragraph below, then fill in the information in the chart

Save the Moon Bears

In the legend of Hwan-ung, a bear prayed to become a human and gave birth to Tan-gun, the first king of Korea. While bears are important to Korea's culture, today they are in great danger. The moon bear, which has a white V shape on its chest, is very popular in traditional Chinese medicine. Because of this, some farmers keep moon bears in tiny cages and drain the liquid in their gallbladders(쓸개) to sell mostly to oriental medicine doctors in China and elsewhere. There are very few of these beautiful bears living in Jiri-san, so we must rescue the bears in farms to save the species. We must help save these wonderful animals and protect our culture!

Topic sentence: ____________________

Supporting detail 1: ____________________

Supporting detail 2: ____________________

Supporting detail 3: ____________________

Exercises

Exercise 4.4

Replace some of the nouns with pronouns to avoid repetition.

1. I talked to Sarah yesterday. Sarah said that the test was really difficult.

2. Opium was one of the most important trade goods in the 1800s. Today opium is a component of organized crime and terrorism.

3. One of the first popular reality TV shows was COPS. COPS showed real police officers fighting crime in a different city each week.

4. In my opinion, global warming is the most serious problem facing the world today. Global warming affects everything from food to war and may soon kill millions of people.

5. Michael used to play basketball when he was in high school. In university though, Michael doesn't play basketball because he has a part-time job.

6. Yoko Ono is often seen as the person who destroyed the Beatles. However, Yoko Ono deserves credit as an influential artist.

7. Yesterday was very cold. Yesterday was also the first day of spring.

8. Some people think that the Great Wall of China is Asia's most important landmark. I think, however, that the Great Wall of China is not as impressive as Angkor Wat.

9. Ji-eun made spaghetti for lunch. However, Ji-eun said the spaghetti was not great.

____

10. Green tea is a traditional drink in Asia. Recently, however, green tea has also become popular in the West because green tea has many health benefits.

____

Unit 05 The Writing Process

Objectives	- Learn the Writing Process - Brainstorming - Using an Outline

The Writing Process

There are many ways to approach writing. Good writing is almost always the result of a strong, clear process, a step by step guide to walk you through the effort. Different books and authors may use different words to describe each step and divide the parts differently, but all include some kind of process. In this course, we will use a five step process and see how to put a paragraph together. In this course, we will use a five step process and see how to put a paragraph together.

Pre-writing	-	determining the subject, generating ideas, making notes
Planning	-	creating a topic sentence, making an outline
Drafting	-	writing the first draft
Editing	-	looking for mistakes and problems
Revising	-	fixing the mistakes and rewriting the paragraph

Pre-writing

In this step, we get ready for our writing. First, we need to know the basic subject of our paragraph. Often, your instructor or professor will assign your topic. Other times, you will need to choose a subject. Now, by subject, we don't mean your topic sentence. Here we are referring to the general idea that we'll be covering. The subject is general, covering many possible topics. The topic sentence is specific, focused on one thing.

Look at the example on the next page. Maybe your instructor says, "Write a paragraph about travel." The subject "travel" is very large. You could write about many things. You could write a paragraph about the best trip you've taken, your dream vacation, the cost of plane tickets, good places to visit in Paris, and so on.

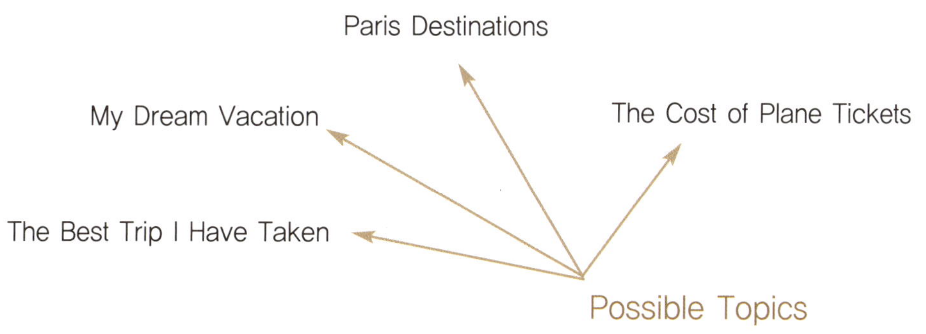

Travel is general, 'My Dream Vacation' is specific. At this stage in the writing process, we just need the subject. If the instructor gives you a subject, you're ready to continue. If you don't already have a subject, then you will need to pick one. Usually you will want something you enjoy or find interesting. If you pick something boring, you won't want to do the writing and you will probably receive a lower grade than you hoped.

Also, when you select your subject, make sure you know if you will be writing a descriptive paragraph – telling the reader about something – or a persuasive paragraph – trying to change people's opinions or actions. Knowing what kind of paragraph you will write will help you select the subject. Some subjects are better for descriptive paragraphs, while other subjects are better for persuasive paragraphs.

Once you have a subject selected, you will need to think about possible topic sentences. Again, sometimes you will be told what the topic is directly. More often, though, you will need to figure out your topic by yourself. If you are having a difficult time deciding on a topic, brainstorm.

Brainstorming can be done in many ways. The typical way is to write the subject in the middle of a piece of paper and then write down as many ideas about the subject, no matter how strange, silly, or unusual it might be. After you finish writing down your ideas, group them together and look for ideas that are related.

Planning

Now it's time to make a plan. Many students make the mistake of just starting to write. Bad idea! Unless you are really lucky, you will probably write something that is confusing or requires a lot of editing later. If you take some time to plan, though, you can usually do a much better job writing your paragraph.

There are many ways to plan, and every writer will develop his or her own method, using whatever ways are best for them. For now, let's focus on the traditional outline. An outline is very similar to a blue print that an architect makes to build a house or building. Without a blueprint, the building can't be built properly. Without an outline, your writing may be confusing, messy, or incomplete.

Topic sentence: *Write your topic sentence here.*

I. the first main detail goes here
  A. *information about the first main detail is added here*
    1. *if there are sub-details about (A), write it here*
      i.
      ii.
      iii.
        a.
        b.
    2. *and here*
  B. *and here*

II. the second main detail goes here
  A. *information about the second main detail is added here*
  B. *and here*
  C. *and here*

III. the third main detail goes here
  A. *information about the third main detail is added here*
  B. *and here*

Mate

Drinking *mate* is an important cultural activity in Paraguay, Argentina and southern Brazil. The tea is drunk through a metal straw from a large cup, which is passed from person to person. People in this part of South America believe that *mate* helps to relax the mind and keep the body cool. Furthermore, because *mate* is always shared, drinking it builds friendships between people. As you can see, *mate* is an essential part of South American life.

Topic sentence: drinking *mate* is an important cultural activity in Paraguay, Argentina and southern Brazil.

I. How it is drunk
  A. Metal straw
  B. Passed person to person

II. Why is it drunk
  A. Relaxes mind
  B. Keeps body cool

III. Other information
  A. Always shared
  B. Builds friendships

Exercise 5.1

Arrange the five steps of the writing process in the correct order.

__ Editing
__ Drafting
__ Pre-writing
__ Planning
__ Revising

Exercise 5.2

Which step of the writing process does each sentence below represent?

revising	pre-writing	editing	drafting	planning

__________ In this step, you write the first, rough draft of the paragraph.
__________ Now you will fix the problems you found in the previous step.
__________ Brainstorm ideas for the subject.
__________ In this step, you will write the topic sentence and prepare an outline.
__________ Look for mistakes such as misspellings and grammar problems.

Exercise 5.3

Think of five ideas for each of the topics below.

School

____
____
____
____
____

Exercises

Travel

Getting a Job

Fashion Trends

Exercise 5.4

Look at the brainstormed ideas below. Group them together in logical groups. Give a subject name for each group. There may be some unused items.

programs CSI news TV stars
dramas Kim Joon EBS
bad for children
Sony
LCD American shows **Television** Korean TV shows
Yoon Eun-hye

Friends OnStyle MBC SBS Kim So-eun
Educational shows police dramas Sex and the City
Cartoons Boys Over Flowers
Love Story in Praha game shows reality TV sitcoms
waste of time couch potato Samsung
LG KBS OCN Goo Hye-sun Lee Min-ho
Song Ji-hyo Winter Sonata

Group 1

Group 2

Group 3

Group 4

Exercise 5.5

Using the four groups you made from exercise 5.4, write a topic sentence for each.

Group 1 ______________________________

____

Group 2 ______________________________

____

Group 3 ______________________________

____

Group 4 ______________________________

____

Exercise 5.6

Write the Roman numeral for each number below.

A. 4 ______

B. 7 ______

C. 10 ______

D. 2 ______

E. 13 ______

F. 50 ______

G. 63 ______

H. 100 ______

I. 29 ______

J. 246 ______

Exercise 5.7

Arrange the items below in the correct order to make a proper outline.

3 B I 1 A ii i C 2 1 i ii iii 2

___

    ___

        ___
        ___

            ___
            ___

___

    ___

        ___
        ___
        ___

    ___
    ___

Unit 06 | Choices, Choices, Choices

Objectives

- Choosing supporting details
- The Rule of Three
- Writing the first draft
- Editing for mechanics

The Writing Process Continued

The third step of the writing process is drafting. In this step, the goal is to write the first version of the paragraph. To do this, you need your outline from the second step. Turn your outline into a paragraph by taking the keywords and phrases and making them into sentences with signal words. Add a summary and a closing statement at the end, and of course an opening statement at the beginning.

So, how many sentences will you have to write? There is no specific answer for that. The very minimum for this kind of paragraph is four, but that would almost certainly not be a strong paragraph. In most cases, you will write one or two introductory sentences to prepare the reader for what you are going to talk about, or to get the reader intercested. Then one sentence for the topic sentence. The first supporting detail needs at least two sentences in most cases, and maybe three or four. The same is true for the second supporting detail, though it usually has the least amount of explanation. The third supporting detail is often the biggest or most important detail, so you may need three, four, or five sentences to explain it. A summary sentence or two is usually included. And whatever you say at the end, your goodbye message to the reader, will take one or two sentences.

As you can see, this gives us between eleven and seventeen sentences. So let's say that ten sentences would be the minimum in most cases, and twenty would be a lot, almost too many. When a paragraph gets longer than fifteen sentences, many people would prefer to break it into smaller pieces. Therefore, we should try to stay under twenty sentences if we can.

Drafting Checklist

1. Title
2. Introductory sentence(s)
3. Topic sentence*
4. Supporting detail #1*
5. Explanation of detail #1*
6. Supporting detail #2*
7. Explanation of detail #2
8. Supporting detail #3
9. Explanation of detail #3
10. Summary sentence(s)
11. Ending statement*

Editing

Mechanical Edits	Logic Edits	Style Edits
Spelling mistakes	Factual errors	Word order
Punctuation errors	Inaccurate data	Word choice
Capitalization errors	Vague(unclear)	Order of supporting details
Subject-verb agreement mistakes	Unconvincing examples	Poor introduction
Verb tense mistakes	Confusing	Poor conclusion
Word form errors (adjective/adverb)	Doesn't support topic sentence	Just doesn't work
Block style (using new lines)	Doesn't belong in paragraph	
Missing indent		
Missing word		

Editing for Mechanics

When we edit for mechanics, it's very common to use symbols, especially if you are editing another person's writing. Take a moment to look at the editing marks in the table on the next page. There are many different marks used in editing. The ones shown are just some of the most common.

	Insert a period (comma, question mark, etc)		Capitalize/make lower case
∧	Insert a word, letter, etc		Delete the word
	No space needed between two words		Check the spelling, or don't abbreviate
	Delete this letter		Change the word order
	Insert an apostrophe (quote, double quote, accent mark)	T	Wrong verb tense used
→|	Indent	WC	Word choice, use a different word

Exercise 6.1

Which details belong to which topic? Match them accordingly.

Topics

a) My favorite vacation was a trip to Paris when I was twelve.

b) In my opinion, we need to stop using plastic.

c) There are several reasons to study abroad.

d) Admiral Yi Sun-shin is Korea's greatest hero.

Details

__ bad for the environment
__ can't be recycled easily
__ more cultural understanding
__ very special time for my family
__ really delicious food
__ better chance to learn languages
__ created the turtle ship
__ make great friends
__ can be toxic
__ inspired his soldiers
__ won every battle
__ many famous sites

Exercise 6.2

Find the spelling mistakes in these sentences. Write the correct spelling below the word.

1. On Wensday, Professer Baek gave a lecture on the Berlin Airlift.
2. Hellow? I'm your neghbor. Can you pleas turn the volumn down on the radio?
3. Their was nothing good on televison last night.
4. In my opinoin, we should do more to stop globel warning.
5. Cristmas will fall on a Sunday this year.
6. Chaple class is a requred coarse for freshmen.
7. You should go to bad early tonite.
8. Her name was writen on the envalope.
9. The assingment is do on Septimber eighten.
10. We heared a wierd niose outside the window.

Exercises

Exercise 6.3

Correct these common word choice mistakes.

1. Please correct you're mistakes.
2. Their are some oranges in the kitchen if you want them.
3. Who's shoes are these?
4. The teacher called they're parents.
5. Your coming with us tomorrow, right?
6. Now than, let's talk about tomorrow's test.
7. Its time to study, not play.
8. I don't no, maybe we should ask the professor weather these is right answer.
9. I hope the Bears don't loose the game tomorrow.
10. I am not sure where Hannah and Chulwon are; there supposed be here now.
11. I don't think the whether will effect our plans very much.
12. This is you're fault, not mine.
13. The dog was angry that the cat was drinking from it's water bowl.
14. Its clear that we need a medical school at our university.
15. Sohee had more to drink then Kelly.
16. These pants are too lose; I need a smaller size.
17. The financial crisis had many affects.
18. Your sure there going to help us move this weekend?
19. The Security Council did not know weather their actions would have any affect.
20. Rather then change there strategy, many banks continued bying mortgage securities.

Exercise 6.4

Fix the problems with ending punctuation in the following sentences.

1. Really. Are you sure!
2. Oh my goodness?
3. Help. Call the police.
4. Can you do more to help save the environment!
5. There are two ways to solve this problem!

Exercise 6.5

Fix the problems with subject-verb agreement in the following sentences.

1. Dayoung are a very diligent student.
2. Soongsil University were founded by Christian missionaries.
3. The cat sleep all day.
4. An apple a day keep the doctor away.
5. You is from Australia?
6. He go to Japan tomorrow.
7. Tomorrow's class have been cancelled.
8. They was not happy about the new plan.
9. Minji and Wonho live in the dormitory, but Dahee live at home.
10. What do the doctor need know about my medical history?

Exercise 6.6

Change the verb in parenthesis into the correct tense.

1. The exam __________ __________ on Thursday. (be)
2. I __________ my homework before class. (finish)
3. When I was young, I __________ in the Philippines. (study)

Exercises

4. She _________ _________ when the phone rang. (eat)
5. Maria _______ _______ _______ on her project for several weeks now. (work)
6. This _________ my favorite movie. (be)
7. When Hanbyeol saw the sunrise, he _________ very lucky. (feel)
8. If you want to get a good score, you will need _________ _________ very diligently. (prepare)
9. Polar bears _______ _______ _______ for a few decades now. (endanger)
10. European exports _______ _______ _______ for a long time but now are growing at a steady rate. (decline)

Exercise 6.7

Correct the capitalization mistakes in these sentences..

1. Sally's Birthday party is scheduled for saturday, october 15th.
2. while jesus Christ is the central figure for protestants, catholics and other christians, Many people don't know that he is considered a prophet in islam and can even be found in some hindu beliefs.
3. Well, That was interesting.
4. Frank asked If I knew what the homework was for professor Smith's class.
5. i usually buy my groceries at homeplus, or maybe costco.
6. His favorite Whiskey was jameson, a famous irish brand.
7. The child was reading harry potter and the philosopher's stone by j.k. rowling.
8. Ban ki mun was the first korean to be the secretary general of the United nations.
9. The u.s.s. arizona was one of the many Ships sunk by the japanese In the attack on the u.s. naval base at pearl harbor, Hawai'i.
10. Last Night we watched inception on dvd.

Exercise 6.8

Correct the punctuation errors in the following sentences.

1. Well Im not sure.
2. Tiffany Beth and Seulgi went to the noraebang after the party.
3. The office is in Arlington Virginia USA.
4. Dr. Choi said You shouldnt drink any alcohol while youre taking this medicine.
5. We ordered the French quiche it wasnt very good.
6. A large strange red bump appeared on Jaeyoungs arm.
7. When I was in school we would sometimes skip class to go fishing near Henrys farm.
8. Mercury pollution in the environment causes many problems birth defects mental problems skin problems and many other illnesses.
9. Thats mine the prince shouted at the thief but it was too late he had escaped over the wall.
10. Late one night last summer Mallory made an amazing shocking revolutionary discovery.

Unit 07 | # Planning Makes Perfect

Objectives

- Editing for logic
- Editing for style
- Personal pronouns, formal versus informal language
- Avoiding common mistakes

Editing for Logic

Logic, in writing, refers to how well the topic sentence is supported by the information that follows. Good logic is absolutely essential in persuasive paragraphs. If you want to change someone's opinion, you have to convince them with strong reasons that make sense to them.

In descriptive paragraphs, logic refers to how well the details explain or illustrate the topic sentence. You've probably heard the expression "A picture is worth a thousand words." The reverse is also true. Good descriptive writing should help the reader SEE what you are talking about.

Editing for style is difficult, because it is often just how you feel about the writing. There are some things that we can look for. First, we should consider the person. 'Person' here refers to whether you use "I", "you", "we", "one" or "they". It may not seem like that big a deal, but, in fact, it's actually pretty important. There is considerable difference between first person singular and third person. In many cases, you want to connect with the reader on a personal level, so we can use I and you, as though author and the reader are having a conversation. This is good for casual writing and some persuasive paragraphs. In more serious writing, and especially for academic writing, using third person is absolutely required. This creates a little bit of separation between the writer and reader, but it also makes your writing sound more authoritative, more accurate, and perhaps more believable. When you use "I", the reader might just think that the writing is your opinion. If you use "it" and "one", the reader might feel that the paragraph is based on facts and analysis. Read both paragraphs at the top of the next page.

1st Person Singular	I	1st Person Plural	We
2nd Person Singular	You	2nd Person Singular	You
3rd Person Singular	One, He, She, It	3rd Person Plural	They

No GMO!

In my opinion, genetically modified organism food should be banned. When we eat GMO food, we are exposed to strange genes and chemicals. Scientists tell us that these are safe for us, but they are too new. How can we know for sure that they aren't affected us? Furthermore, when we plant GMO vegetables, they can be eaten by insects and animals, or spread to other fields. This gets the modified genes into more of the environment, making the world more dangerous to us. Therefore, I want the government to ban GMO!

No GMO!

Genetically modified organism food should be banned. When people eat GMO food, they are exposed to strange genes and chemicals. Scientists say that these are safe for humans, but they are too new. It is impossible to be certain that they won't affect people later. Furthermore, when farmers plant GMO vegetables, they can be eaten by insects and animals, or spread to other fields. This gets the modified genes into more of the environment, making the world more dangerous to everyone. Therefore, the government should ban GMO!

In the first paragraph, it feels like the writer is talking to us as we read, as though she is giving us her thoughts directly. In the second paragraph, we get the impression that the writer is calmer and maybe more knowledgeable.

If you are writing a report or essay for a class, don't use "I". For these forms of writing, third person is required. Scientists and researchers will use "we" in some cases, meaning either "their team of researchers" or "the entire community of scientists". If you are not sure whether to use first person or third person, use third person.

Things to be careful using in school or academic writing

- Curse words
- Slang
- Jargon
- Foreign language words

Exercises

Exercise 7.1

Fill in the chart with personal pronouns.

	Singular Pronoun	Possessive	Object	Plural Pronoun	Possessive	Object
1st						
2nd						
3rd male female neutral	 he ______ ______	 his ______ ______	 him ______ ______			

Exercise 7.2

Choose the proper preposition from the box to fill in the blanks..

of	in	on	by	to	until

1. If you are going ___ the store, can you buy some milk, please?
2. Sam's birthday is ___ Friday.
3. The first incident occurred ___ April.
4. The Statue ___ Liberty is one of the most famous landmarks in the USA.
5. You have ___ next Wednesday to finish the assignment.
6. They were reading Les Misérables ___ Victor Hugo.

Exercise 7.3

Rewrite the paragraph without using first and second person pronouns.

Seat Belts Save Lives

When you ride in a car, do you use the seatbelt? In my opinion, we should always wear a seatbelt when we are in a car. I have several reasons for this opinion. First, seat belts save lives. You have a one in five chance of getting into a car accident. According to statistics I found on James Madison University's website, 35,000 people die each year in the United States. What was shocking, I think, is that fifty percent of those people could have lived if they wore a seatbelt. Secondly, I learned that car accidents are responsible for most of the brain and spinal cord injuries. These kinds of injuries are easily avoidable if you wear a seatbelt. Finally, the website I visited said that most children who die in a car accident are killed by an adult who is not wearing a seatbelt. So, for me it is clear, you must wear a seatbelt for yourself and for your family. Next time you get in a car, buckle your seat belt!

Exercise 7.4

Fill in the blanks with *like*, *such* as, *for example*, and *for instance*.

1. India has many interesting holidays __________ the Festival of Diwali.
2. There have been many monster sightings around the world. __________, in Scotland, many people claim to have seen a dinosaur in Loch Ness.
3. Many delicious fruits grow in Malaysia __________ rambutans, papaya, and starfruits.
4. Can you get some groceries, __________ butter and some vegetables for a salad, please?
5. Scientific discoveries can happen by accident. __________, penicillin was discovered when Alexander Fleming accidentally dropped some moldy bread into a petri dish of bacteria he was studying.

Exercise 7.5

Do these words need to be translated or transliterated? Write them in English in the most appropriate way.

1. Eunseon is giving a 가야금 recital tomorrow at the Art Hall. __________
2. I'm really hungry; let's have 돈까스 for lunch. __________
3. The children were playing with a 방패연 in the park. __________
4. This restaurant is famous for their fresh 초밥. __________
5. In modern times, women will still wear a 한복 on special occasions like weddings and holidays. __________

Exercise 7.6

Rewrite these sentences to make them more formal.

1. You wanna go to Lotte World tomorrow?

2. There're a whole lotta reasons for saving money.

3. I dunno, what'd ya wanna do?

4. There's gotta be a better way to do this.

5. You should of gotten more sleep, you know?

Exercise 7.7

Match the informal words on the left with their formal synonyms on the right.

big	items
get	acceptable
see	many/much
you	children
kind of	somewhat
stuff	have
kids	one
OK	large
lot of	observe

Unit 08

Putting it All Together

Objectives

- Review key lessons
- Walk through the paragraph writing process
- Prepare to write a descriptive or persuasive paragraph

Review

The 6 Rules of Paragraphs

1) The first sentence is indented.
2) The first letter and proper names are capitalized.
3) Every sentence ends in punctuation (. ? !).
4) Each sentence has a subject and a predicate, or main, verb, and they match each other in voice and number (subject-verb agreement).
5) All sentences are about one main idea.
6) Sentences do not start on new lines.

Titles

In many cases, you will need to put a title at the top of your writing. When we write a title, capitalize the first letters of all nouns, verbs, adjectives and adverbs. You do not need to include quotations or other punctuation around it.

✓ A Tale of Two Cities.

✗ "a tale of two cities"

✗ 〈A tale of two cities〉

✗ A TALE OF TWO CITIES

The Writing Process

Pre-writing – determining the subject, generating ideas, making notes
Planning – creating a topic sentence, making an outline
Drafting – writing the first draft
Editing – looking for mistakes and problems
Revising – fixing the mistakes and rewriting the paragraph

Plagiarism

Copying the work of others is strictly forbidden. Using someone else's writing as if it were your own is called plagiarism. In Western universities, there are very severe punishments for students who are caught cheating in this way. While it might be very easy to find something to use on the Internet, you must avoid this kind of activity.

Exercises

Exercise 8.1

Review topic sentences from earlier units, then write two strong topic sentences for each subject, one descriptive and one persuasive.

1. University entrance exam
   (descriptive) ______________________________
   ____
   (persuasive) ______________________________
   ____

2. Learning English
   (descriptive) ______________________________
   ____
   (persuasive) ______________________________
   ____

3. China
   (descriptive) ______________________________
   ____
   (persuasive) ______________________________
   ____

4. Fashion trends
   (descriptive) ______________________________
   ____
   (persuasive) ______________________________
   ____

5. Bill Gates
   (descriptive) ______________________________
   ____
   (persuasive) ______________________________
   ____

Exercise 8.2

Fill in the outline with the information from the box.

I. ____________________
  A. How do you get around your city?
  B. ________________________________

II. ____________________
  A. __________________________
    1. ______________________________
      i. Town bus = 800w
      ii. ______________________________
    2. Subway costs
      i. ______________________________
    3. T-money card discount = 100w
  B. __________________________
    1. ______________________________
    2. Buy ticket
    3. Signs are clear and easy to read
  C. __________________________
    1. Many bus stops
    2. ______________________________
    3. Transfers between bus and subway = free
    4. ______________________________

III. ____________________
  A. Seoul's public transportation good, cheap, easy to use, convenient
  B. __________________________

Use transport card
Introduction
Bus costs
Conclusion
Body
"In my opinion, Seoul has a great public transportation system."
Cheap
Try it!
convenient
easy to use
9 subway lines and suburb lines
iPhone apps, electronic signs
1000w/10km
City bus = 1000w

Exercises

Exercise 8.3

Use the outline you finished in exercise 8.2 to write the paragraph.
Make a good title for the paragraph.

Exercise 8.4

Re-read the paragraph you wrote in exercise 8.3. Look for any mistakes you might have made. Use the checklist below to help you.

	Structural Edits
☐	All sentences end with either . ? !
☐	All sentences have a subject and verb; subject-verb agreement (I go, she goes)
☐	The first word of every sentence, proper names, and abbreviations are capitalized. Check for problems with for *I, it, if, in, and is.*
☐	Each new paragraph is indented.
☐	There are no fragments or clauses without sentences. Check any sentence that starts with *Because*, *Since*, or *So* to be certain it is okay.
☐	Plural nouns are used when referring to general things. *(I like kittens. Students need to study.)*
☐	*They're, their, there* are all used correctly.
☐	*For example, for instance, like*, and *such as* are used correctly.
☐	Adjectives and nouns are not confused. *(She has an ~~activity~~ **active** personality.)*
☐	Pronouns are used instead of repeating nouns. (The monkey is in the tree. ~~The monkey~~ It is very cute.)

Paragraph Assessment

Use these pages to help prepare for your paragraph assessment.
Your instructor should provide you with a topic for your paragraph.

Follow these steps as you start working on your paragraph.

Step 1 Pre-writing

- ☐ Get topic from instructor
- ☐ Brainstorm ideas about topic
- ☐ Narrow your focus

Step 2 Planning

- ☐ Write a topic sentence
- ☐ Create a brain map
- ☐ Complete an outline

Step 3 Drafting

- ☐ Write the first (rough) draft

Step 4 Editing

- ☐ Don't look at the essay for at least one day
- ☐ Read the essay carefully
- ☐ Mark any mistakes, typing errors, or other problems; make notes as you read

Step 5 Revising

- ☐ Fix the mistakes from Step 4
- ☐ Write next draft of the essay
- ☐ Repeat Step 4 and 5 until you have a perfect draft

Step 1 Brainstorm

Topic (from instructor): ______________________________

Step 1 Narrow Your Focus

Look again at the ideas you wrote on the brainstorm page. Group similar ideas together and write them here. You may not need all the groups or lines.

Group 1

Group 2

Group 3

Group 4

Other ideas that don't fit in your groups:

Step 2 Write a Topic Sentence

Subject (from instructor): ______________________________

Review the subject from the instructor and read through your brainstorming and focus notes. Based on these factors, write a topic sentence. Generally, topic sentences are your opinion about the subject. In many cases, you should be able to write "In my opinion…", "I believe that…" or "There are several reasons why…" in front of your topic sentence.

Examples

In my opinion, we must do more to stop global warming.
There are several reasons why Google will be the most powerful technology company in the world soon.
I believe that respect is the most important aspect of a healthy marriage.
I believe that practice with native speakers is the only way to really learn a language.

Topic Sentence: (In my opinion / I believe that / There are several reasons why…)

____

Three supporting details:

Detail 1 ______________________________

Detail 2 ______________________________

Detail 3 ______________________________

Step 2 Create a Brain Map

Use this page to help visualize your paragraph.

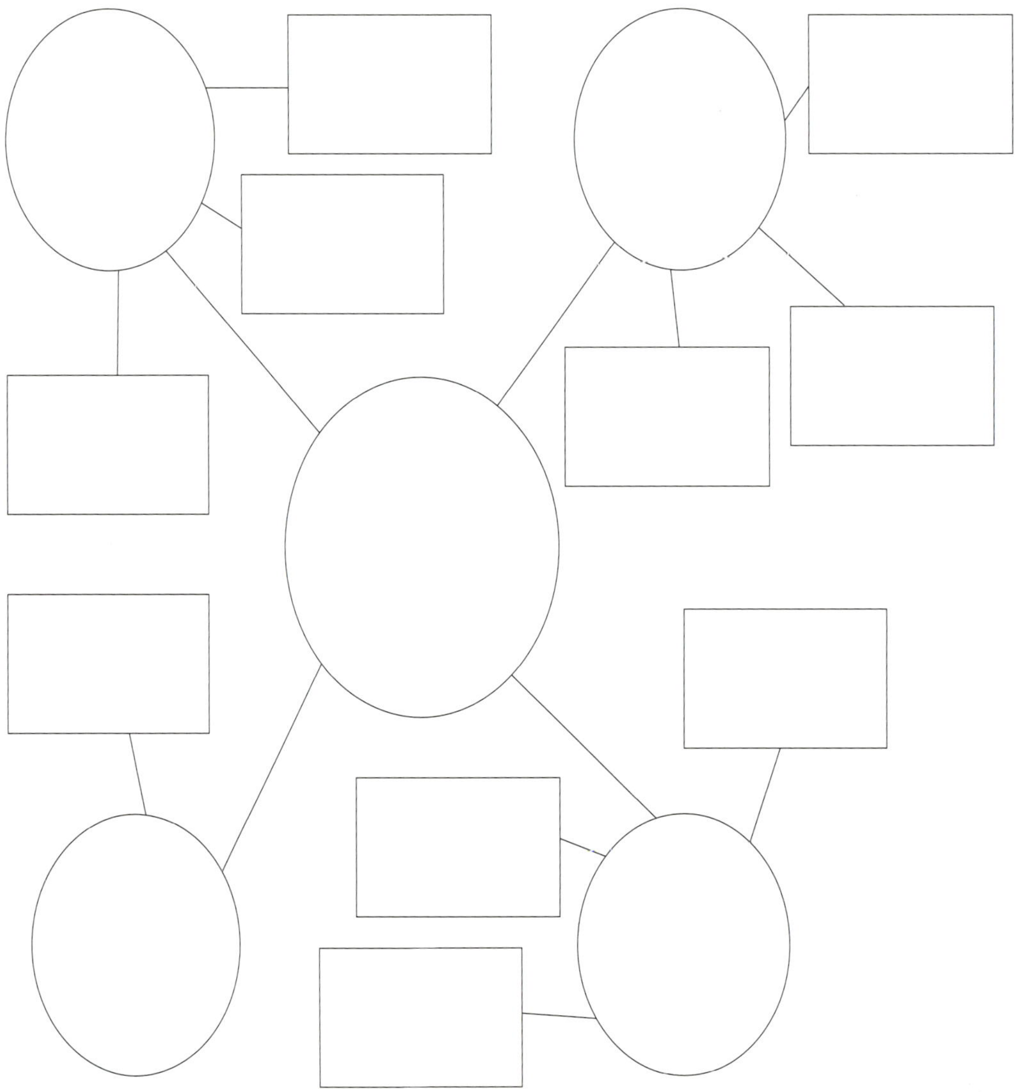

Step 2 Complete an Outline

Use the following pages to create your outline. Remember, you do not need to write complete sentences in your outline; key words and phrases, facts and figures are sufficient. You should, however, write your topic sentence and any direct quotes from other people in full sentence form.

There are many lines for details and sub-details. You may not need all of them. Use only those that you need. Add more if needed.

I. Introduction

A. (opening statement)________________________________

i. ________________________________

ii. ________________________________

B. (topic sentence) ________________________________

C. Preview

i. (detail 1)________________________________

ii. (detail 2)________________________________

iii. (detail 3)________________________________

II. (Detail 1) ________________________________

A. ________________________________

i. ________________________________

ii. ________________________________

B. ________________________________

i. ________________________________

ii. ________________________________

C. ________________________________

i. ________________________________

ii. ________________________________

III. (Detail 2) ________________________________

A. ________________________________

i. ________________________________

ii. ________________________________

B. ____________________

i. ____________________

ii. ____________________

C. ____________________

i. ____________________

ii. ____________________

IV. (Detail 3) ____________________

A. ____________________

i. ____________________

ii. ____________________

B. ____________________

i. ____________________

ii. ____________________

C. ____________________

i. ____________________

ii. ____________________

V. Conclusion

A. (summary)____________________

B. (challenge)____________________

C. (memento)____________________

Additional notes for your essay

Paragraph – first draft

In the space below, write the first draft of the paragraph you have been planning on the previous pages. Do not worry about making mistakes. The first draft does not need to be perfect. Focus on developing your ideas and support for your topic sentence.

____________________ (title)

Step four – editing

Now you will read through your paragraph and look for mistakes.
Use the checklist below to help you with this process.

	Structural Edits		Logical Edits
☐	All sentences end with . ? !	☐	The topic sentence is strong and easy to understand.
☐	All sentences have a subject and verb; subject-verb agreement (I go, she goes)	☐	The introduction is interesting to the reader.
☐	The first word of every sentence, proper names, and abbreviations are capitalized. Check forproblems with *I*, *it*, *if*, *in*, and *is*.	☐	The title is clear, strong, related to the lo the paragraph.
☐	Each new paragraph is indented.	☐	Every sentence is directly related to the topic sentence.
☐	There are no fragments or clauses without sentences. Check any sentence that starts with *Because*, *Since*, or *So* to be certain it is okay.	☐	Facts, statistics, and other factual data have the source listed *(According to the Oxford Dictionary⋯)*
☐	Plural nouns are used when referring to the to general things. *(I like kittens. Students need to study.)*	☐	Details are interesting and related to the topic.
☐	*They're*, *their*, *there* are all used correctly.	☐	The supporting ideas are arranged in the best order (strongest last, chronological, etc)
☐	*For example*, *for instance*, *like*, and *such as* are used correctly	☐	The conclusion has a summary of the main ideas.
☐	Adjectives and nouns are not confused. *(She has an ~~activity~~ **active** personality.)*	☐	The conclusion has a strong closing statement (memento).
☐	Pronouns are used instead of repeating nouns. (The monkey is in the tree. ~~The monkey~~ It is very cute.)		

step five – revising | second draft

Using the list of problems you discovered in step four, rewrite your paragraph. This second draft should be much better than the first draft.

Repeat step four with this second draft. When you have read it several times and can find no more mistakes, write or type the final draft and give it to your instructor.

Name__________ Number__________

Fall Semester

Foundation of Freshman English Writing

Unit 09 Reviewing the Basics

Objectives

- Review the Six Rules of Paragraphs
- Practice writing fundamentals

Paragraph Elements

There are several elements to a paragraph. At the very top, you can see the title. Generally, we put a title at the top of our writing, for paragraphs and essays. After the title, the next thing we see is the topic sentence. The topic sentence is an essential part of this style of writing. We use it to tell the reader what the purpose of the writing is. It clearly states the main idea and tone or feeling of the writing. Usually, the topic sentence shows the author's opinion about the subject.

The largest part of a paragraph or essay is the body. The body explains in detail the author's main idea. The details needed to show what the author means or the supporting evidence to prove the author's argument in a persuasive essay. In a descriptive essay, the body contains many sense details – how something feels, sounds, tastes, looks, smells – and facts about the subject. In a persuasive essay, the body uses statistics, quotes, analysis, examples and other data to prove that the author's opinion is correct.

Finally, you can see the conclusion. Naturally, the conclusion's job is to conclude the writing. There are many different ways to do this. Often, the conclusion offers the reader a summary of the topic sentence and main points from the body. Many authors like to give the reader a final thought or something specific to remember about the writing. In a persuasive essay, you might want to tell the reader to do something specific – if your writing is about saving the environment, you might end by asking the reader to turn off extra lights and appliances at home. In general, you should not introduce any new information in the last paragraph.

Fair Trade Coffee (Title)

Do you like coffee? I do. I drink coffee every day. (Opening statement)
But I now only buy fair trade coffee. (Topic sentence)
Recently I learned that many coffee shops buy their beans from large companies that do not support their workers well. In fact, many of these companies keep their costs low by using children to do the hardest work. Fair trade coffee comes directly from the coffee farmers; no large companies earn money from the farmers' work. (Body) Next time you want a cup of joe, please order fair trade coffee. It's the right thing to do. (Conclusion)

The Six Rules of Paragraphs

1) The first sentence is indented.
2) The first letter of every sentence and proper names are capitalized.
3) Every sentence ends in punctuation (. ! ?).
4) Each sentence has a subject and a main verb, and they match each other in voice and number (subject-verb agreement).
5) All sentences are about one main idea.
6) Sentences do not start on new lines.

Exercises

Exercise 9.1

Rewrite the sentences below with proper capitalization.

1. an african bee flew into becky's room.

____

2. The New Store In coex Mall Had A Sale On Jeans.

____

3. on wednesday lieutenant kim took the ktx to busan.

____

4. steven went to the pc room in bongcheon to copy jong-su's Japanese music dvd.

____

5. for her english class won-hee has to read "one hundred years of solitude."

____

6. The doctor from chungang university hospital was eating at quizno's in gangnam.

____

7. i just bought a christian dior dress for the oscars ceremony in California next april.

____

8. kim yuna is one of the most famous korean athletes, especially after the beijing Olympics.

____

9. Finally, It is clear that we need to find a way to save palau and the Maldives from sinking below the pacific Ocean.

____

10. gretchen was born in Switzerland but moved to sydney, Australia when she was nine.

____

Exercise 9.2

Correct these titles.

1. “Bee Season”

   ____

2. 〈Crime Scene Investigators〉

   ____

3. The jewel in the palace

   ____

4. The First Shop Of The Coffee Prince

   ____

5. for whom the bell tolls

   ____

6. A brief history of time

   ____

7. Hedwig And The Angry Inch

   ____

8. Zen and the art of motorcycle maintenance

   ____

9. ‘Super Mario Brothers’

   ____

10. Pride And Prejudice

    ____

Exercises

Exercise 9.3

Identify the topic sentence in these paragraphs.

Seat Belts Save Lives

When you ride in a car, do you use the seatbelt? In my opinion, we should always wear a seatbelt when we are in a car. I have several reasons for this opinion. First, seat belts save lives. You have a one in five chance of getting into a car accident. According to statistics I found on James Madison University's website, 35,000 people die each year in the United States. What was shocking, I think, is that fifty% of those people could have lived if they wore a seatbelt. Secondly, I learned that car accidents are responsible for most of the brain and spinal cord injuries. These kinds of injuries are easily avoidable if you wear a seatbelt. Finally, the website I visited said that most children who die in a car accident are killed by an adult who is not wearing a seatbelt. So, for me it is clear, you must wear a seatbelt for yourself and for your family. Next time you get in a car, buckle your seat belt!

Fair Trade Coffee

Do you like coffee? I do. I drink coffee every day. But recently I learned that many coffee shops buy their beans from large companies that do not support their workers well. In fact, many of these companies keep their costs low by using children to do the hardest work. Children should be in school. That's why I now only buy fair trade coffee. Fair trade coffee comes directly from the coffee farmers; no large companies earn money from the farmers' work. Next time you want a cup of joe, please order fair trade coffee. It's the right thing to do.

Save the Moon Bears

In the legend of Hwan-ung, a bear prays to become a human and gave birth to Tan-gun, the first king of Korea. While bears are important to Korea's culture, today they are in great danger. The moon bear, which has a white V shape on its chest, is very popular in traditional Chinese medicine. Because of this, some farmers keep moon bears in tiny cages and drain the liquid in their gallbladders(쓸개) to sell mostly to oriental medicine doctors in China and elsewhere. There are very few of these beautiful bears living in Jiri-san, so we must rescue the bears in farms to save the species. We must help save these wonderful animals and protect our culture!

Exercise 9.4

Find sentences that are unrelated to the topic sentence.

A Tragic Day

September 17th, 1862 was the single bloodiest day in United States history. On that day, near the town of Sharpsburg along Antietam Creek 23,000 men died fighting in the American Civil War. On September 11th, 2001, only 3000 people died, so Antietam was worse. The leader of the Southern Army, General Robert E. Lee had begun an invasion of the Northern States as part of the Maryland Campaign. The Northern leader, Major General George McClellan, had many more troops than Lee, but due to poor strategy failed to defeat the Southern army. In that day of the Battle of Antietam, more Americans were killed than in any other battle in the nation's history.

Exercises

Exercise 9.5

Rewrite this paragraph in the proper block style. Don't forget to indent.

____

____

____

____

____

____

____

____

____

____

____

____

____

____

____

____

____

For the Children

My granddaughter is six years old.
She loves to play with her friends and draw pictures.
But, she does not have much time to do these fun things because she goes to an English kindergarten at 9am every day.
After she returns home at three pm, she meets a Korean tutor for an hour, and then she goes with her brother to tae-kwon-do class.
Why do our children have to study so much?
When do they have time to be children?
By the time they reach university, they are tired of studying.
Our children cannot and should not endure so much stress.
We MUST look at ways to change the education system so that children have a chance to be children.

Exercise 9.6

Correct the subject-verb agreement problems in these sentences.

Some students was late. ________

The answer are wrong. ________

A mother and her baby was crossing the street. ________

Money and information is important in the global economy. ________
Tae-sub don't do his homework. ________
Alicia and Ji-yeon wasn't at the meeting. ________
Tomorrow the weather are going to be awful. ________
If you drinks too much soju, you will be sick tomorrow. ________
The new teacher want to learn all the students' names. ________
There are a table and lamp in the bedroom. ________

Exercise 9.7

Unscramble the sentences. Add the proper punctuation(. ! ?) as needed.

1. the landed flower butterfly A on

   ____

2. a teacher of homework gave The lot

   ____

3. bus Stephanie her missed

   ____

4. hand the please me Can book, you

   ____

5. some you tired If drink are coffee

   ____

6. a my Oh It's god bee

   ____

7. restaurant know Do is where you the

   ____

8. me Please help

   ____

9. do We it can try if we

   ____

10. don't where restaurant I know is the

    ____

Unit 10

Odds & Ends : Parts of an Essay, Grammar, Signal Words

Objectives

- Identify the parts of an essay
- Look at various grammar problems
- Learn about signal words

Essays follow the same basic structures we learned for paragraphs. They have an introduction, a body, and a conclusion. The roles of each of these parts are the same as well. The introduction gets the readers' attention and tells them what the essay is about. The body explains the author's opinion or the details about the subject; and the conclusion summarizes the main points and lets the readers' go with something to remember.

Introduction →

Do you like fast food? I do, and I'm sure most of you do too. But recently, I've tried to stop eating fast food entirely. There are several reasons for this decision. Fast food isn't healthy, it's bad for children, and it is bad for the environment. Let me explain these reasons in more detail.

Body →

Firstly, fast food isn't healthy. Most meals at popular chains like McDonald's and Lotteria have high amounts of sodium and considerable amounts of calories. Sodium can lead to heart disease and high blood pressure. Likewise, high calorie meals cause obesity and even diabetes. These are all serious health concerns. Furthermore, fast food companies target children with ads, special meals, and toys. These practices ensure that children become hooked on fast food from a very early age. Finally, the industry is bad for the environment. Fast food chains need massive amounts of meat. Raising cows and chickens takes up lots of space which damages forests and grasslands, and the animals produce tons of toxic waste as well as greenhouse gases. Some experts believe cows might be one of the worst polluters on the planet.

Conclusion →

In conclusion, there are many reasons why I decided to stop eating fast food. It's unhealthy, it targets children, and it destroys the environment. I would like you to join me in breaking our addiction to fast food. Even if you just avoid it during the weekdays, it would be a good start. Fast food will probably always be with us, but it doesn't have to be such a big part of our lives.

The roles of each part are the same as we saw with paragraphs. The introduction catches the readers' attention and tells the readers what the writing is about. The body explains in detail the reasons or arguments supporting the main idea of the writing, and the conclusion summarizes the writing and lets the readers go with something to remember or think about.

We learned in the previous course that a topic sentence is needed when we write a paragraph. In an essay, however, we have a thesis statement. The thesis statement acts like a topic sentence, but it is the main idea for the entire essay, not just a paragraph. Try to find the thesis statement now.

Thesis statement : But recently, I've tried to stop eating fast food entirely.

Transitions

One of the essential parts of essays is the use of transition or signal words. These words help the reader move easily from one idea to the next, and to understand how each idea connects to the others. These signal words help the reader follow the ideas in the essay by showing where one thought finishes and the next one starts, and how each thought connects to the others in the essay.

Firstly, fast food isn't healthy. Most meals at popular chains like McDonald's and Lotteria have high amounts of sodium and considerable amounts of calories. Sodium can lead to heart disease and high blood pressure. Likewise, high calorie meals cause obesity and even diabetes. These are all serious health concerns. Furthermore, fast food companies target children with ads, special meals, and toys. These practices ensure that children become hooked on fast food from a very early age. Finally, the industry is bad for the environment. Fast food chains need massive amounts of meat. Raising cows and chickens takes up lots of space which damage forests and grasslands, and the animals produce tons of toxic waste as well as greenhouse gases. Some experts believe cows might be one of the worst polluters on the planet.

There are many categories of signal words that have different roles.

Sequence: first, second, third, firstly, initially, finally, then, next, before, after, meanwhile
Comparison / Similarity: likewise, similarly, also, comparatively, by the same token, as well as
Contrast / Difference: on the other hand, but, however, conversely, instead, by contrast, rather
Additional: in addition, furthermore, moreover, plus, additionally

Conclusion: in conclusion, thus, finally, So, in the end, therefore, in summary, to sum up, as you can see
Opinion: in my opinion, I think, I believe, I hold that, it is my belief that
Examples: for example, like, for instance, such as
Cause / Effect: therefore, thus, so, as a result, due to, if... then, accordingly, since, because (of)

These are just some of the many transition words available to us when we are writing an essay. It is essential that we use these; otherwise an essay will be difficult to understand and feel strange to the reader. Look at these examples:

Cause/Effect
Choppy: The balloon had a whole in the surface. It began to come down.
Smooth: Because the balloon had a hole in its surface, it began to come down.

Additional Information
Awkward: Kimchi is a traditional dish beloved by almost every Korean.
It has antioxidants that may help fight cancer.
Smooth: Kimchi is a traditional dish beloved by almost every Korean.
In addition, it has antioxidants that may help fight cancer.

Contrast/Difference
Hard to understand: High tax rates may have a negative impact on consumer spending.
They give the government more resources for social welfare.
Clear: High tax rates may lower consumer spending.
On the other hand, they give the government more resources for social welfare.

Essential Grammar

Every sentence in an essay should follow good grammar rules. Some parts of grammar, though, seem to often cause students difficulty. The first one is subject-verb agreement. You may recall, the main verb of a sentence must match the subject of the sentence in number and voice. What this means is, you might have to change the verb if the subject is plural or in second or third person.

Examples of Subject-Verb Agreement

Present			
I am a student.	*You are a student.*	*She is a student.*	*We are students.*
Past			
I was a student.	*You were a student.*	*She was a student.*	*We were students.*
Perfect			
I've been a student.	*You've been a student.*	*She's been a student.*	*We've been students.*

This rule about subject verb agreement also applies to clauses and phrases within sentences too.

Examples of Subject Verb Agreement in Dependent Clauses

*Since Sohee **was** late, she had to sit in the back of the classroom.*
*Since Sohee and Jun-bin **were** late, they had to sit in the back of the classroom.*

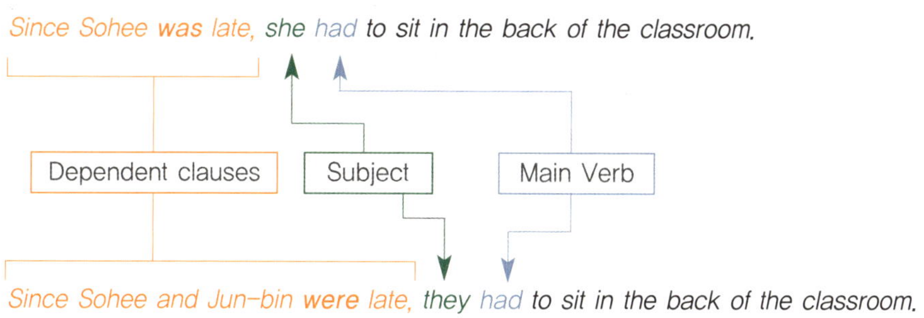

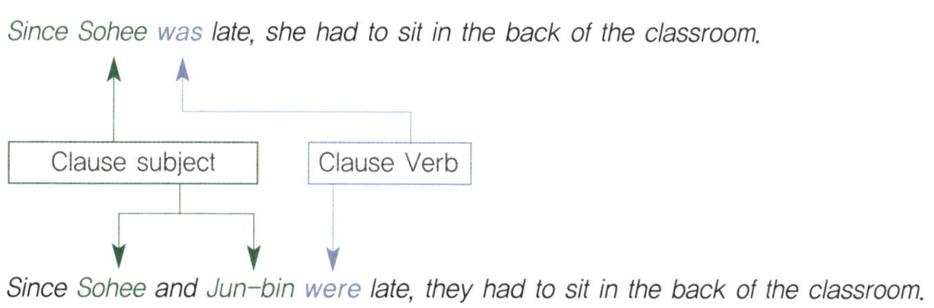

Exercises

Exercise 10.1

Underline the clauses (subordinate, dependent, relative) in each sentence.

1. According to the news, it will snow tomorrow.
2. When we first came to school this building wasn't finished yet.
3. Because I was late, I missed the quiz.
4. Sarah didn't know who was knocking on the door.
5. Families are hurting because of the economic recession.
6. Since the price increased last month, people are buying fewer heads of cabbage.
7. Meet me where the bus stops.
8. Anyone who lives in Gyeonggi-do should be able to live in the dorm.
9. Listening to her iPod, Claire didn't hear the phone ring.
10. In my opinion taxes are too high.

Exercise 10.2

Write these signal words in the correct box.

Continuing a Thought	Contrast

Opening	Concluding

Confirmation	General Use.

Confirmation

consequently
clearly, then
and
to be sure
as soon as
moreover
later
besides that
following this further
meanwhile
also
in the light of the... it is easy to see that
on the other hand
yet
soon
nevertheless
in the first place
on the contrary
obviously
certainly additionally
of course
undoubtedly
in addition
hence
in final analysis
in conclusion
in final consideration
indeed

Exercises

after, afterwards
at first, at last
before, before long
finally
because
no doubt
first... second... third
however
in the meantime
admittedly
therefore
but
unquestionably
next
furthermore
in the same way
then

Exercise 10.3

Do you need the simple present, simple past, or simple future tense?

1. Tomorrow, we ________ to the park. (go)
2. The boss ________ last week. (resign)
3. The cat always ________ in the window. (sleep)
4. If you ________ red wine, you have to be careful about staining your teeth. (drink)
5. The new car ________ on electricity instead of gas. (run)
6. Before we ________, she was dating a musician. (meet)
7. Green ________ the big color for this fall. (be)
8. Hello Kitty ________ one of Japan's most popular characters. (be)
9. Jeongmin ________ he ________ to your party next Sunday. (say / come)
10. I ________ for the test so probably I ________ a bad grade. (not study / get)

Exercise 10.4

Change the verb to the proper form of the continuous tense.

1. I ________ my grandmother next month. (see)
2. They ________ about the lecture when they left the classroom. (talk)
3. The classes ________ late tomorrow because of the snow. (start)
4. When you ________ the flour in the water, mix continuously. (add)
5. If students ________ in the hall, they should be quiet. (wait)
6. The president ________ a special announcement next Friday. (make)

Exercise 10.5

Change the verb to the perfect tense.

1. They ________ many changes to the proposal, but it's still not perfect. (made)
2. She ________ French for many years. (study)
3. By the time the average student graduates, he ________ more than 28 million won. (spend)
4. He ________ the movie already so he didn't want to come to the theater with us. (see)
5. If humans continue using fossil fuels at the current rates, we ________ all the known supplies of gas and coal by the year 2075. (use up)

Exercise 10.6

Identify each part of the essay below.
Parts: introduction, body, conclusion

The other day my family and I wanted to visit my wife's family farm in Gangwondo. We jumped in the car and started our drive. Eight hours later, we finally arrived, exhausted and annoyed. It was non-stop traffic all the way there!

Exercises

Driving in and around Seoul is even worse. Going to work by car is almost impossible, so usually I take the subway, even though the station is far from my house and my job. I believe it is time for the government to begin taxing cars heavily. There are three reasons for this proposal: taxes will discourage people from purchasing cars, it will raise income for the government to spend on roads and transportation, and it encourages people to use public transportation.

If something costs a lot, most people can't buy it. That is a simple fact. Right now, cars are too cheap, so almost anyone can buy a car if they want it. Many families in Seoul have two cars now. However, there is no room on Seoul's streets for these cars. Unless there is a heavy tax on cars, people will keep buying too many. Of course, this will be difficult for poor families that might need a car for work, so the government could make a tax that affects rich people more than poor people. Further, the government will have to give some benefit to car makers like Hyundai and Kia; perhaps a tax break for them, or some other consideration would make it more acceptable.

Money from taxes helps the government provide for the people of the nation. With more taxes from cars, the government can improve the road and highway system. Larger and better highways between Seoul and the provinces would be especially useful. Bus lanes could be added to even more streets to improve the public transportation system. Or perhaps the tax money could be used to expand the KTX system, with new lines to Seocho and other cities that are currently difficult to reach. As long as the new tax money is used wisely to help the traffic and transportation system, then the people will feel a great benefit from the tax.

Finally, a tax as I've proposed will encourage people to use subways, trains and buses, because if fewer people buy cars, more people will need to use public transportation. There are many benefits from this. First, it will reduce traffic on the streets, of course. Second, it will preserve the environment, since public transportation is much more energy efficient than cars. Third, it makes the transportations more profitable and allows them to improve and expand their services. As we all know, the subway system especially needs to remodel many of their stations; so if they have more customers, they will have more money to fix their problems.

Therefore, for these three reasons, I want the government to propose a new tax on car sales. Such a tax will improve traffic conditions, raise money for road and transportation systems, and encourage use of buses and subways which have many advantages. Please help me to support this proposal by emailing, calling, or writing letters to members of the National Assembly. Send letters to the local newspapers. Post this message to your blog or homepage. If we work together, we can improve our country!

Exercise 10.7

Answer these questions about the essay above.

1. What is the essay's hook?

____

2. What is the essay's thesis statement?

____

3. What are the three main points to support the thesis?

____

____

____

4. What is the essay's challenge?

____

5. What is the essay's memento or closing statement?

____

6. Find ten signal words in the essay.

____

Unit **11** | # Ideas & Organization

Objectives

- Comparatives and Superlatives
- Organizing ideas in a paragraph

Comparisons and Superlatives

Comparing one thing to another requires specific ways of using adjectives. If you are comparing two separate things or groups of things, you will need to form the comparative of the adjective. When comparing one thing to all of the other things, then you need the superlative.

The Comparative

The comparative is formed by adding -er(-ier for -y words) or *more* to an adjective. Short adjectives add the suffix-er to the end; most adjectives that are two or more syllables use the word *more* before the word.

Examples

Juhyun is taller than Seulgi. *tall + er*

This apple is juicier than those. *juicy - y + ier*

I think that Gojae Island is more interesting than Jeju Island. *more + interesting*

Frank got a better grade on the test than we did. *~~good~~ better*

The weather is worse than we expected. *~~bad~~ worse*

The Superlative

The superlative is made in the same way as the comparative except it uses *-est* and *most.* Also, in most sentences, you will need the word the or a possessive noun before the adjective.

Examples

Juhyun is the tallest woman in the class. *the + tall + est*

This is the juiciest apple I've ever eaten. *the + juicy + iest*

I think that Gojae Island is Korea's most interesting vacation spot. *Korea's + most + interesting.*

Frank got the best grade on the test. *the + ~~good~~ best*

The weather is the worst we could have imagined. *the + ~~bad~~ worst*

Now take a look at this essay on pets. Notice the use of comparisons and superlatives.

Do you have a pet? If so, what kind is it? If not, what kind would you want? Personally, I have a dog and a cat, but I think dogs are the best kind of pet. There are several reasons for this opinion.

First, dogs are more fun. They love to run around and chase things. You can throw a stick or ball and a dog will run after it and bring it back to you. Have you ever tried that with a cat? A cat might chase the ball, but good luck getting it back. Cats are best at catching mice, but overall dogs are more exciting. Dogs are much more playful and are more energetic playmates.

Secondly, dogs are smarter, usually. Animal trainers agree, dogs are easier to train than cats. Also, dogs can remember more commands and can understand more commands. They learn faster than cats, too. Cats can learn some tricks and commands, but most breeds of dogs are more intelligent.

Finally, dogs are more loving. Dogs come from wolves and wolves live in large packs, so dogs are more familiar with living in groups. Cats are loners, so cats are the best at living on their own. Dogs are more sociable; they need others around them. When I come home, my dog is more excited to see me. My cat only cares about me if I have some food for her.

So, I think dogs are the best pets. Cats are best at some things, but dogs are better companions. Dogs are better friends than cats. If you are looking for a pet that will love you, get a dog.

Organization

There are many ways to organize information in an essay: cause and effect, problem and solution, chronological, sequential, strongest first, strongest last, geographical, and so on. Very early in the writing process, you will want to consider how you will organize your essay, so let's take a look at some of the organizational styles.

Cause & Effect / Problem & Solution

We often want to examine what makes something happen, or how something came to be the way it is. Or perhaps you will want to write about a problem facing society today and the ways to solve that issue. With these two styles, you will divide your essay into four parts: introduction, cause/problem paragraph, effect/solution paragraph, and conclusion. Topics that work well in this style include: global warming, unemployment and poverty, obesity, scientific processes, government policies, and other topics the deal with issues that need explanation.

Keep in mind, you almost never use the words I, me, or my in this kind of essay. This kind of essay usually deals with facts and analysis. The thesis statement might be your opinion, but we usually don't say "I think," or "in my opinion" in Cause/Effect or Problem/Solution essays.

Introduction
↓
Cause/Problem
↓
Effect/Solution
↓
Conclusion

Signal Words for Cause&Effect / Problem&Solution Essays

- as a result
- because
- therefore
- due to
- if...then
- leads to
- thus
- certainly
- possibly
- initially, lastly, finally

Examples

Thesis statement: *Human activity is the leading cause of global warming.*

Body Paragraph 1: *The causes of global warming:*
transportation, manufacturing, large-scale farming

Body Paragraph 2: *The effects of global warming:*
species extinction, natural disasters, sickness and disease

Chronological / Sequential

Next we'll look at the chronological or sequential essay. In this kind of writing, you write about things in order from first to last, oldest to newest, earliest to latest and so on. In some ways, this might be the easiest organizational style and certainly it can be used for many kinds of writing: instructional, how-to pieces, historical reports, explanations of process, and many more.

When writing this style of essay, you might consider the Rule of Three, or in other words, having three main supporting points for your thesis. Having 3 points is a very common and very effective technique.

Introduction
↓
Support #1
↓
Support #2
↓
Conclusion
↓
Support #3

Signal Words for Chronological and Sequential Essays

- initially, lastly, finally
- first, second, third
- firstly, secondly, thirdly
- then
- next
- before, after
- meanwhile
- as
- at the same time
- simultaneously
- during
- following
- in (date)
- previously

Examples

Thesis statement: A tangled series of events led to first World War.

Body Paragraph 1: For 75 years, European nations had been forming complicated, often secret, treaties and alliances

Body Paragraph 2: The assassination of Archduke Ferdinand and the Austro-Hungarian Empire's response

Body Paragraph 3: With each new country entering the war, more alliances and treaties were triggered, engulfing the entire world in conflict

Strongest First / Strongest Last

In many cases, you will choose three main details or examples to support your thesis statement. When these details are not in any sort of obvious sequence, then you will need another way to arrange the details. The two most common strategies are 'strongest first' and 'strongest last'. That is, look at the three details you are going to use and determine which is the longest or most important. When that detail is needed to understand the other two, put it first. If the other two details lead to the most important one, put it last. Generally but not always, 'strongest last' is the better method.

Introduction

↓

Second strongest detail

↓

Smallest detail

↓

Strongest detail

↓

Conclusion

Signal Words for Strongest First/Strongest Last Essays

- initially, lastly, finally
- first, second, third
- firstly, secondly, thirdly
- furthermore
- in addition, additionally
- moreover
- like wise
- for example, such as, for instance
- similarly
- also
- in conclusion
- therefore
- thus
- so

Examples

Thesis statement: University tuition should be lowered.

Body Paragraph 1: Students have to work part-time jobs or take a year off to earn money

Body Paragraph 2: Schools don't use the money effectively and don't reveal where the money goes

Body Paragraph 3: It places a huge burden on families, especially families with many children, with many negative consequences for society

Exercise 11.1

Choose the right adjective for the sentence and change it to the comparative.

interesting	sad	expensive	hard	lazy	diligently
good	bad	cold	high	spicy	

1. January is ______ than February usually.
2. Your food is ______ than mine.
3. I think it was raining ______ yesterday.
4. ______ taxes will discourage people from smoking.
5. The iPhone is selling ______ now than it was last year.
6. Even though he studied ______ for the test than Becky,
   he got a ______ grade.
7. The book was ______ than the movie, in my opinion.
8. She liked the ______ bag but she couldn't afford it.
9. The students were ______ this semester than last.
10. He thought watching TV would cheer him up, but it just made him ______.

Exercise 11.2

Choose the right adjective for each sentence and change it to the superlative.
Don't forget to use "the" if it is needed.

runny	deadly	difficult	beautiful	funny	lazy
low	good	bad	delicious	good	disgusting

1. Gina is ________ person in our class; her jokes make everyone laugh.
2. Of all the places I've traveled, Cambodia was ________.
3. Oh no! This is ________ score I ever got on a test!

Exercises

4. You should try the carbonara; it's ________ item on the menu.
5. She won the Grammy for ________ new artist of the year.
6. Ebola is one of the world's ________ viruses.
7. She said Saw was ________ movie she ever saw.
8. According to different celebrity gossip sites,
   Lady Gaga is either ________ or ________ dressed singer in America.
9. Jim told us that the Welsh accent is ________ to understand for many people.
10. Don't eat there; their eggs are ________ in town.

Exercise 11.3

Make a comparison between the items listed below. Use full sentences.

1. Eiffel Tower / The Louvre

   ____

2. KTX / flying

   ____

3. Ferrari / Porsche

   ____

4. Gucci / Armani

   ____

5. Love / hate

   ____

6. Girls' Generation / Wonder Girls

   ____

7. China / USA

   ____

8. Starbucks / Angel-In-Us

____

9. Pepero Day / White Day

____

10. You / your best friend

____

Exercise 11.4

Which organization style would be best for each essay?
Choose: strongest last, chronological, cause/effect, or problem/solution

______ 1. Thesis: In my opinion, we need to worry less about appearances.
Body: psychology research, ethical behavior, benefits for society.

______ 2. Thesis: Making delicious Christmas fudge is not difficult.
Body: steps one through seven.

______ 3. Thesis: Traffic is a serious problem in our city, but there are some solutions.
Body: too many cars, no space for more roads; London-style congestion toll in city.

______ 4. Thesis: Lack of sleep can happen for many reasons and has several effects on our body and health.
Body: what causes sleeplessness; the results of sleeplessness.

Unit 12

Begin at the Beginning

Objectives	
	- To explore essay introductions in detail - To learn about hooks - To make a good thesis statement - To learn about previews/roadmaps

Parts of an Introduction

As you may remember from the spring semester course, there are three parts to the introduction. First, there is the hook. Then there is the thesis statement, which is like a topic sentence for the whole essay, and finally, there is a preview of the essays main points.

The Hook

Hooks are sentences that make the reader want to read the essay. In many cases, a hook is unnecessary; the topic sentence is interesting already. But probably most essays can use a hook effectively. There are several styles of hooks.

The Question

Starting your essay with a question is an easy and effective way of getting the reader interested in your writing. When you ask a question at the beginning of the essay, the reader will usually think about the answer and then naturally read on looking for the writer's answer too.

> Questions are easy, but can be boring. If you start every essay "Have you ever...?", readers (or your instructor) will get really bored.

The Anecdote

One of the most powerful hooks is the anecdote, or personal story. This could be a small example from your life, or from someone you know, or even something you've seen or heard about from another source. Personal stories make the reader very interested, especially if the story relates to the reader somehow. If their experience is similar to the author's, the reader will feel a connection with the writer and want to read more.

> Make sure the story directly relates to the topic sentence.
> If you use a personal story, it should be an example of what you are talking about in the essay.

The Surprising Fact

"Something in your refrigerator can kill your entire family! Find out tonight on the nine o'clock news!" We hear and see the surprising fact quite often in advertising. It works very effectively because people will be worried or startled and want to learn more about the subject. These can be used well for certain essays and certain topics.

> When you use this hook, it must be true!
> You can't lie just to get the audience's attention.

The Joke

People love to laugh. If you can make the readers laugh, they will be eager to read your writing. The joke has to relate to the essay directly. You can't just say something funny just to make people laugh; your hook must always connect with the topic sentence.

"I'm going to begin with a joke so we can get the humor out of the way."

> Do not try to use a joke if you aren't funny!
> A bad joke is a terrible hook.

Other Styles

There are many other ways that a essay can begin. In some cases, a definition might work. A quotation from a famous person can be useful in many situations. No matter what you use, the important thing to remember is "BE INTERESTING!" No one wants to read a boring essay!

The Thesis Statement

Similar to a topic sentence, the thesis statement tells the main purpose of the essay, directs all the paragraphs that follow, and usually states the author's opinion about the subject.

Examples

In my opinion, university tuition is too high.

There are many factors a student should consider when choosing a major.

I think that we all have a responsibility to fight global warming.

Studying abroad will change your life forever.

Spring is my favorite season.

The Battle of Stalingrad played a major role in weakening the German army.

The Preview

After you tell the reader what the overall subject of the essay is, you will usually want to give them an idea about the main points you are going to make to support your thesis statement. This is called the preview or road map. In some cases, you might have the preview in the thesis statement. Most of the time, though, it will be in its own sentence or maybe in a few sentences, one for each main point.

Examples

Thesis Statement | Preview

In my opinion, university tuition is too high.
It puts a burden on families, forces students to get part-time jobs, and doesn't benefit the students.

There are many factors a student should consider when choosing a major.
First, she should think about her interests. Secondly, she needs to consider her strengths and weaknesses. Finally, she will want to think about her dreams.

I think that we all have a responsibility to fight global warming.
There are several reasons for this opinion. First, we all are the cause and the solution. Second, the problem is too big to fight if we aren't all working together. Third, everyone will share in the benefits.

Studying abroad will change your life forever *because it will open your mind to new experience, introduce you to new friends, and teach you to be self-reliant..*

Spring is my favorite *season because it is a time of rebirth, it has my favorite holiday – Easter – and the weather begins to warm up.*

The Battle of Stalingrad played a major role in weakening the German *army in many ways: militarily, financially, and spiritually.*

You start by writing something interesting that will make the reader want to continue reading, then you tell them the main idea of the essay, which is often your opinion about the subject, and finish with a sneak peek at the main points or arguments that you will write about in detail in the body.

Exercises

Exercise 12.1

Mark the hook, the thesis statement and the preview in these introductions.

1. What's your earliest memory? For me, it was walking through a grassy field in a park on a bright spring day. I was three and I got stung by a bee on my arm. Most importantly, according to my mom, it never happened. Memory is a mysterious, amazing thing. In this essay, I will explain how the brain forms memories, how memory changes over time, and how false memories occur.

2. When the Church forced the astronomer Galileo Galilee to say that the Earth does not revolve around the sun, he sent secret letters to other scholars telling them about his discoveries. Galileo was just one of many scientists whose voice had been silenced by religious and political organizations. There are many reasons why this happens. Religious leaders worry that discoveries will challenge people's faith. Political leaders fear losing power. Finally, people generally dislike change.

3. "Shaken, not stirred." If you've ever seen a James Bond movie, you've heard this famous line as the international spy orders a martini. Martinis are a classy drink and anyone can look sophisticated ordering one. In this essay, I'll tell you about the martini's history, the different kinds of martinis, and how to make your own at home.

Exercise 12.2

Select a hook for each of these theses

1. In my opinion, birds should not be kept as pets.

   A. How many different birds can you think of?

   B. Maya Angelou's most famous poem is "I Know Why the Caged Bird Sings".

   C. There are few things more amazing than watching a hawk or eagle gliding through the skies high above the earth.

2. Making a delicious pizza is easy and fun.

   A. What's your favorite Italian dish?

   B. Almost everyone loves pizza, but delivery and store-bought pies are just not good enough for a true pizza lover.

   C. Have you ever tried a New York or Chicago style pizza?

3. There are several things you should watch for when buying a notebook computer.

   A. Many people find the stress of buying a new computer takes away the joy of getting a new device.

   B. When was the last time you bought a new computer?

   C. Are you a super-user or are you computer illiterate?

4. The Mona Lisa is the most famous painting in the world, but few people know why.

   A. Have you ever visited the Louvre?

   B. The first time I saw the works of Van Gogh, I was inspired to become an artist.

   C. If I ask you to think of a painting, chances are you will imagine the Mona Lisa.

5. It may be a cliché, but there is some truth to the saying 'laughter is the best medicine'.

   A. Which would you prefer, a shot of antibiotics or a good joke?

   B. Laughter releases several hormones into the brain.

   C. Knock, knock? Who's there?

Exercises

Exercise 12.3

Which of these would be a good thesis statement for the subject?
Match the thesis with the subject and type

1. Subject: volunteering — Essay type: persuasive ___
2. Subject: volunteering — Essay type: descriptive ___
3. Subject: global warming — Essay type: persuasive ___
4. Subject: global warming — Essay type: descriptive ___
5. Subject: healthy relationships — Essay type: persuasive ___
6. Subject: healthy relationships — Essay type: descriptive ___

A. In my opinion, the government and industries must reduce carbon emissions.
B. I learned about healthy relationships by watching my parents.
C. Every student should do volunteer work before they graduate.
D. One of the most valuable lessons I learned in university was not in the classroom, it was from volunteering.
E. Before you can love someone else in a lasting and healthy way, you have to love yourself.
F. The conflict in Darfur may be one of the first wars begun due to global warming.

Memo

Unit 13 | Supporting the Thesis

Objectives

- Exploring the body of an essay
- Choosing details and arguments
- Referencing outside sources

In the last lesson, we talked about the introduction as the first impression of a new boy or girl on a blind date. You get an idea of who the person is and what they want or think from your first sight of them and the first bits of conversation, just as you learn the subject, specific topic, and main points of the essay from the introduction.

The body is more like the next few dates with that new boyfriend or girlfriend. You learn more about their life and personality through talking and spending time together. In an essay, each paragraph gives you more insight into the author's thinking, his or her opinions and how they want us, the reader, to understand the topic of the essay.

When you wrote the introduction, if you did a good job, you got the reader's attention with an interesting hook; then you told the reader what the essay is about and possibly your opinion on the topic with the thesis statement. Finally, you told the reader what the major points you are going to make to support or prove your thesis statement with the preview.

Now, you have to actually support the thesis as you promised you would in the preview. In unit 3, we talked about organizing details, and you may want to take a look through that again. We'll also look at strong supporting details versus weak ones, and how to use data and information from other sources. With any luck, by the end of this unit, you should have a good idea about how to write the body of an essay.

The Body

Cheers!

Anyone who visits Korea quickly learns how to drink soju. Korean drinking culture is very interesting with its many rules and rituals. Likewise, other countries have their own special drinks and drinking culture. Learning about these special liquors and drinking cultures can be a very fascinating experience. In this essay, we will discover how and what the Russians, Germans, and the Irish drink.

First, let's look at Russia's love affair with vodka. Vodka is a strong, clear liquor made from potatoes or grain. For over 500 years, Russians, the Polish, and Ukrainians have been drinking "the water of life" and since the 1950s, it has become one of the most popular alcohols in the world. In most countries, people drink it in cocktails, like the White Russian, but in the so-called "vodka belt" – Russia, Poland, the Ukraine – it is drunk "neat", meaning with nothing else, not even ice. Similar to Koreans, Russians like to eat when they drink vodka; this is called *zakuvski*. If you are drinking with Russians and you finish the bottle of vodka, you should put it on the floor or next to the table leg. An empty bottle on the table looks like the drinkers are poor and may bring bad luck. Don't forget to say "Budem zdorovy".

As you might guess, Germans love beer. They <u>really</u> love beer. Germans are among the heaviest drinkers in Europe. You may have heard of Oktoberfest. This is an 18 day long festival that starts in September – it is based on an old calendar – for the sole purpose of celebrating beer. The festival is especially popular in Munich; the Munich Oktoberfest is the largest folk festival in the world. At the festival, you can order special brews from Munich's six breweries. Before drinking, make sure everyone at the table is ready, then clink the glasses together on the bottom of the *krug* – German for beer glass – and shout *Prost!*

If you go to most large bars in the world, you will almost certainly find Guinness on tap. This distinctively dark, thick beer is Ireland's most famous drink, but the country also produces some of the best whiskeys as well. Besides having excellent alcohols to choose from, Ireland also has a distinct pub culture. Irish men and women will often gather in local 'public houses' to spend time with neighbors and coworkers in a relaxed atmosphere. Musicians playing traditional Irish music will often play in the evening, or older folk might share long, usually hilarious stories. When you cheer with Irish friends, be sure to say ***sláinte***.

As you can see, there are many ways to enjoy alcohol around the world, from vodka with Russians to beer with Germans to whiskey with the Irish. Next time you want to wet your whistle, why not try something from another culture? Cheers!

This essay is a traditional five paragraph descriptive essay. How many main points does it use to support its thesis statement? As we've talked about before, this essay uses three major supporting details. Each of these three main points has several details as well. Stylistically, the three body paragraphs are similar to each other. They start by introducing the country's representative alcohol, then give some detailed information about the drink and end with some tips about drinking in that country. Because the essay is giving some information and advice to the reader, the author used the 1st person plural – us and we – and the second person – you – to have a kind of conversation with the reader(change the "let's" in 6 and the two "you"s in 8 to bold and different color).

First, let's look at Russia's love affair with vodka. Vodka is a strong, clear liquor made from potatoes or grain. For over 500 years, Russians, the Polish, and Ukrainians have been drinking "the water of life" and since the 1950s, it has become one of the most popular alcohols in the world. In most countries, people drink it in cocktails, like the White Russian, but in the so-called "vodka belt" – Russia, Poland, the Ukraine – it is drunk "neat", meaning with nothing else, not even ice. Similar to Koreans, Russians like to eat when they drink vodka; this is called *zakuvski*. **If you are drinking with Russians and you finish the bottle of vodka, you should put it on the floor or next to the table leg. An empty bottle on the table looks like the drinkers are poor and may bring bad luck. Don't forget to say "Budem zdorovy".**

Choosing Details and Arguments

When you are writing your essay, it's important to choose strong details and convincing arguments. This is why brainstorming is useful; it helps you to come up with lots of ideas. From those ideas, you can select the strongest, not just the first ones that come into your head.

Looking at the brainstorm below, notice which ones the author chose for the essay above and which ones she did not use. So why did she pick those? There might be many reasons for those choices, but there are certain things to consider. One of the most important points is to think about the audience. Who will probably be reading this? In the case of the Drinking Culture essay, the author knew that her readers would mostly be students in her class in Korea, so there was no need to talk about Korean drinking culture: they already know it!

Some things don't really seem related to the topic very well, or don't have enough brothers and sisters to make a good essay. Looking at what's left, we can see that there are several countries and things related to those concepts.

Now that the brainstorm has been narrowed to just countries and their culture, we need to bring it down to just three countries. Japan is close to Korea, so maybe the readers already know about their drinking culture.

So from this we can see a little bit about how to choose supporting details. Each case will be different, but if you think about your readers, and pick things that are related to each other and directly connected to the topic, you are going to be on the right track.

Drinking culture

soju *vodka* *beer* *whiskey* *cocktails* *alcohol content*

sake *anju* *hofs* *bars* *pubs* *taverns*

OB *Guinness* *Cass* *Hite* *Heineken*

Oktoberfest *pilsner* *ale*

hangover *vomit* *soju bomb* *MT*

Germany *Japan* *Russia* *America* *Korea* *France* *Chile* *Australia*

"Gambae!" *"cheers"* *"Gunpai"* *wine* *one shot*

Gangnam bars *Itaewon bars* *pojang-maja* *jongno bars* *Ireland*

Referencing Outside Material

One of the strongest ways to support your thesis is to use material from other sources. These sources can include magazine articles, books, journal articles, news programs, encyclopedias, websites, and many other things. The reason why these sources are strong support for most theses is that they have more authority than we do by ourselves usually. You or I may have an opinion about something, but in most cases, we lack any authority or importance. Who cares what our opinion is? On the other hand, information from experts, journalists, or other sources is much more valuable in most cases than our own thoughts. We can borrow their credibility to make our points stronger and more valuable.

One thing to remember when you use outside sources is to properly cite them in your writing. There are many different styles for referencing material depending on what you are writing and who you are writing for. Often, your instructor will have a particular style he or she prefers. Below we will look at a modified version of MLA that should be useful for most classes.

The author's name is mentioned in the sentence.	According to Smith, we can expect prices to rise in these circumstances (*Wealth of Nations*, p117).
The author's name is not mentioned.	We can expect prices to rise in these circumstances (Smith, *Wealth of Nations*, p117).
Citing a web source	Munich's Oktoberfest is the largest folk festival in the world (http://www.discover-munich.info).

Exercise 13.1

Group the ideas together and choose one of the labels.

Labels					
Transportation Historical sites Dining Shopping Culture					

ideas

fire chicken subway Namdaemun market Korean BBQ COEX Seoul Art Center buses Gyeongbokgung rice porridge Myeongdong Dongdaemun market Namdaemun Leeum Samsung Museum Gahoe Museum ddeokboki Ewha fashion district Changdeokgung Deoksugung kimchi taxis KTX Sejong Art Center

Exercise 13.2

Write down 18 ideas about the subject in the circle

Dreams

Exercise 13.3

Cross out the details that don't belong with the thesis.

1. In my opinion, the government and industry must reduce carbon emissions.
   A. Reducing carbon has many economic benefits.
   B. Carbon can form diamonds under extreme pressure over long periods of time.
   C. Carbon emissions will endanger millions of people in the next several decades.

2. Before you can love someone else in a lasting and healthy way, you have to love yourself.
   A. Scientists have discovered that there are several chemicals in the brain related to love.
   B. Self confidence is necessary for strong relationships with others.
   C. Being unhappy with yourself often makes you unhappy with those around you.

3. There are several things you should watch for when buying a notebook computer.
   A. Price is not the only factor to consider.
   B. Think carefully about what activities you will use your notebook for and how much power they will require.
   C. HP merged with Compaq several years ago, making the new company one of the largest tech companies in the world.

Unit 14 Ending on a High Note

Objectives

- exploring essay introductions in detail.
- learning about hooks.
- making a good thesis statement.
- learning about previews/roadmaps.

Parts of a Conclusion

Only One World

Introduction

Imagine that you and your family live a few kilometers from the beach on a small island. Every year, the ocean is a little closer to your home. One day, the ocean will swallow your home and eventually the whole island. This is more than imagination, it is happening to millions of people in countries like Palau and the Maldives, thanks to global warming. We must act now to stop global warming! There are things we all can do to help: use less electricity, use less fossil fuels, and use less plastic.

...(the body is here)...

Conclusion

So, in conclusion, it is clear that we can and must use less energy, less fuel, and less plastic if we want to save the Earth for our children. When you go home today, turn off lights when you aren't in the room, turn off the TV and other appliances when you aren't using them. Take the bus or better, ride a bike! Doing little things every day can make a big difference. Remember, we only have one world and when it's gone, so are we.

We can see that the thesis statement is "We must act now to stop global warming!" The preview lists three main points: use less energy, use less fossil fuels, and use less plastic. Then if we turn our attention to the conclusion, we can identify three elements. The first element is the summary. The summary's job is to say one more time *in different words* the thesis and main points. This is usually started with some signal words like "in conclusion". The second part is the challenge or call to arms. This is usually only in persuasive essays. It is what the author wants the reader to do or think. The final part is the memento. The memento is a closing statement for the essay. Its job is similar to the hook's; it leaves the reader with something to remember, like a little present. The memento should be strong, interesting, maybe even touching sentence or two or three.

The Summary

Many students find the summary difficult to write. Often they will just say the thesis statement again but with the words "In conclusion" in front of it. While that might do the job, it's not interesting or effective. It is much better if you can say the thesis differently, using different words and maybe emphasizing it in a slightly different way.

Examples

Thesis: In my opinion, chocolate is the best ice cream flavor.
3 main points: It's the most delicious; it has a long and interesting history; chocolate has good physical and mental health properties
Summary: Therefore, it is clear that chocolate's great taste, interesting history, and health properties make it the best ice cream flavor.

Thesis: Freedom of speech is the most important of all human rights.
3 main points: it's the foundation for modern life; it's allows us to protect our other freedoms; we cannot be our true selves without it.
Summary: Thus, freedom of speech is the most essential of our rights because without it we cannot be truly free, especially in the modern age of communication that we live in now.

Thesis: September 17th, 1862, at the Battle of Antietam, was the single bloodiest day in American history.
3 main points: 23,000 soldiers were killed; Union general was too cautious and had poor strategy;
Confederate general had flexible strategy and good positions.
Summary: Thus we can see that due to the Union general's mistakes and the Confederate general's constantly evolving strategies, what should have been a major victory for President
Lincoln resulted in the most American lives lost in one day.

Challenge/Call-to-Arms

As we mentioned earlier, the challenge or call-to-arms is what the author wants the reader to think or do. Naturally, this is mostly used in persuasive essays where the author is hoping to change people's attitudes or actions, or affect government, corporate or school policies. Sometimes you can use a challenge in a descriptive essay too. This works well when you are describing things like vacation spots, fun activities, or for instructional essays about making things or cooking.

Examples

Thesis: In this essay, I will tell you how to make a delicious French quiche.
Challenge: Now you know how to make the quiche, so why don't you do it this weekend?

Thesis: We must ban the use of plastic in restaurants and homes.
Challenge: Please write to your member of the National Assembly and ask them to ban all plastics that come into contact with food.

Thesis: Universities must freeze tuition fee increases.
Challenge: Join us at City Hall next Friday for a candlelight rally to protest tuition increases.

The Memento

The final element of the conclusion is the memento or closing statement. Like we noticed earlier, the way you finish your essay plays a big role in how the reader will remember what you wrote. That's why a lot of authors put a lot of effort into writing a powerful, effective conclusion.

The most common mistake students make is not having any closing statements at all. They just write a summary and finish there. Or they try to say things like "Thank you for reading." But, generally, we don't say thank you. That is really mostly used in presentations, not essays.

There are no specific rules or tricks for writing a good closing statement. You just have to think about your topic and try to write something that is easy to remember and makes the reader feel some emotion.

Examples

Thesis: We must ban the use of plastic in restaurants and homes.

Memento: Every day plastics continue to infect our food, we put ourselves, our children and everyone else in danger. Let's make this a better, safer world for future generations.

Thesis: September 17th, 1862, at the Battle of Antietam, was the single bloodiest day in American history.

Memento: Remembering the sacrifice those young men made in defense of their ideals and their nation should make us pause and think about our own lives. Our small problems and petty arguments seem much less important in that light.

Thesis: Universities must freeze tuition fee increases.

Memento: If we don't fight these increases, the cost to our families and our futures will be much higher than just a few million won. It's time to take a stand against these unfair costs.

Exercises

Exercise 14.1

Match the thesis with its summary.

Thesis

1. In my opinion, seaweed soup is the best cure for a hangover. It has lots of nutrients, plenty of water, and can replace the electrolytes the body loses when you drink. ___
2. People should not wear fur, because it is immoral and the fur industry treats animals badly. ___
3. Smartphones are revolutionizing the way people work, communicate, and play. ___

Summary

A. As you can see, fur should not be worn because of how animals are treated and it is immoral.

B. In conclusion, we can see that work, communication and free time are being transformed by smartphones.

C. So as you can see, seaweed soup is an excellent cure for hangovers because the broth has essential nutrients and electrolytes.

Exercise 14.2

Choose an appropriate challenge for each of the summaries.

1. So as you can see, seaweed soup is an excellent cure for hangovers because the broth has essential nutrients and electrolytes.
   A. Next time you have some drinks, why not have some seaweed soup with your alcohol?
   B. If you want to really enjoy Korean food, you should definitely have some seaweed soup.
   C. If you're drinking this weekend, be sure to have some seaweed soup the next morning.

2. As you can see, fur should not be worn because of how animals are treated and it is immoral.

A. That's why I won't wear fur.

B. Please, share this message with your friends and save the poor animals.

C. There are many other reasons to not wear fur.

3. In conclusion, we can see that work, communication and free time are being transformed by smartphones.

A. Next time you buy a cell phone, get a smartphone.

B. Thus I will get a smartphone soon.

C. Apple and Samsung make the most popular smartphones in Korea.

Exercise 14.3

Choose a memento for each summary and challenge.

1. So as you can see, seaweed soup is an excellent cure for hangovers because the broth has essential nutrients and electrolytes. If you're drinking this weekend, be sure to have some seaweed soup the next morning.

A. You'll be happy you did.

B. Tell me how if it works for you.

C. I think you will enjoy the taste.

2. As you can see, fur should not be worn because of how animals are treated and it is immoral. Please, share this message with your friends and save the poor animals.

A. It's not even that good at keeping us warm.

B. The animals are really cute, too!

C. It's the right thing to do.

3. In conclusion, we can see that work, communication and free time are being transformed by smartphones. Next time you buy a cell phone, get a smartphone.

A. You'll be connected to everyone, all the time, everywhere. Welcome to the future!

B. Or don't, it's your choice.

C. They're good for the world.

Unit 15 | Putting it All Together

Objectives

- Reviewing previous lessons
- Learning about some common mistakes

Now that we've studied all the parts of an essay and walked through the writing process, it's time to get ready for writing your own essay. First, let's review a few things. The foundation of every essay is the paragraph, and each paragraph in an essay follows the same rules. Each paragraph you write on paper or in a word processor software program must be indented. On the computer, you just need to hit the tab key. On paper you should start the first word of the first sentence about five to six letter spaces to the right of the left side of the paper.

Watch your capitalization! The first word of each sentence is, of course, capitalized. All proper names - people, places, buildings, animals, days, months, famous ideas - are capitalized along with most abbreviations, like TV and DVD. Of course, you know that every sentence ends in punctuation. As you know, a sentence must have a subject and verb. The subject and the verb must match correctly; specifically, for words that can be changed with 'he', 'she', or 'it' need an S at the end of verbs in several tenses. "I go, you go, she goes, he goes, it goes, we go, they go." Every sentence in your paragraph must relate directly to the topic sentence. And finally, all the sentences must be in block style; they start immediately after the period from the sentence before, not on a new line.

The 6 Rules of Paragraphs

1) The first sentence is indented.
2) The first letter and proper names are capitalized.
3) Every sentence ends in punctuation (. ! ?).
4) Each sentence has a subject and a main verb, and they match each other in voice and number (subject-verb agreement).
5) All sentences are about one main idea.
6) Sentences do not start on new lines.

Indent

Capitalization

Drinking mate is an important cultural activity in Paraguay, Argentina and southern Brazil.

In my opinion, people need more exercise.

How often do you try something new?

If we work together, we can solve this problem!

Ending punctuation

Paul is an exchange student from Canada.

Subject

Main Verb

Paul and Sarah are exchange students from Canada.

What's your favorite possession? Mine is a pearl necklace that my mother gave me for my 18th birthday. These pearls had been a gift to her when she turned 18 from her mother too. So, they have deep meaning to women in my family. Pearls are ~~formed inside oysters when a piece of sand or something else gets inside their shell.~~ One day I hope to give these pearls to my own daughter.

Unrelated to the topic sentence

✓

What's your favorite possession? Mine is a pearl necklace that my mother gave me for my 18th birthday. These pearls had been a gift to her when she turned 18 from her mother too. So, they have deep meaning to women in my family. One day I hope to give these pearls to my own daughter.

✗

What's your favorite possession?
Mine is a pearl necklace that my mother gave me for my 18th birthday.
These pearls had been a gift to her when she turned 18 from her mother too.
So, they have deep meaning to women in my family.
One day I hope to give these pearls to my own daughter.

The Thesis Statement

One of the very most important parts of an essay is the thesis statement. We know that a topic sentence is the foundation of a paragraph; the thesis statement does the same thing for the essay. Depending on the type of essay you are writing – descriptive, instructional, persuasive – your thesis may be slightly different. A descriptive essay will have a thesis that tells what you are talking about in essay. For instructional essays, your thesis statement will tell the reader what you will teach them. For a persuasive essay, you will write a thesis that contains your opinion about some topic. Look at these examples.

Instructional:

In this essay we will learn how to make traditional kimchi jjigae.

Learning languages is difficult but if you follow these steps, you can learn a little faster.

Descriptive:

Tsar Peter the Great's modernization program dramatically affected Russian society.

My greatest talent is my ability to listen to people.

Persuasive:

In my opinion, "Hamlet" is Shakespeare's greatest play.

Elementary and middle schools should offer more sports for students.

The Body

The body is the meat and potatoes of the essay. This is where all the details and arguments to support your thesis statement go. In general, you need at least one paragraph for each main point in your essay. For longer essays, there might be several paragraphs for each point. In our lesson though, we usually write the traditional 5 paragraph essay.

Inside the body, you will usually put in your opinions and descriptions of things, facts and figures and data from research, analysis of those facts, examples about what you are talking about, and other information that will help the reader understand your subject.

> …
>
> On the other hand, consider the example of TED.org. This conference (which stands for Technology, Education, Design) was first held in Monterrey, California in 1984 and then annually from 1990 through today. While the original purpose reflected its Silicon Valley roots for design and technology, it has since grown tremendously to cover a very wide variety of topics.
>
> According to an article in the Guardian, online videos from various TED or TEDglobal conferences have been watched over 290 million times *(Guardian, TED – the Ultimate in Blue-Sky Thinking, July 4th, 2010).* Through their online outreach, they are trying to make the world a better place.
>
> …

Transition words

Reference

Data

The Outline

We don't need to spend too much longer on the outline. Take a look at this empty outline and see where all the information will go.

I. Introduction

- A. The hook goes here
  1. Details about the hook
  2. Details about the hook
- B. The thesis goes here
- C. Preview of the main points
  1. Main Point 1
  2. Main Point 2
  3. Main Point 3

II. Main Point #1 (usually the 2nd biggest or most important point)

A. Detail about main point 1

1. Specific information
2. Specific information

B. Detail about main point 1

1. Specific information
2. Specific information

C. Detail about main point 1

1. Specific information
2. Specific information

III. Main Point #2 (usually the smallest or least important point)

A. Detail about main point 2

1. Specific information
2. Specific information

B. Detail about main point 2

1. Specific information
2. Specific information

IV. Specific information Main Point #3 (usually the largest or most important point)

A. Detail about main point 3

1. Specific information
2. Specific information

B. Detail about main point 3

1. Specific information
2. Specific information

C. Detail about main point 3

1. Specific information
2. Specific information

V. Conclusion

A. The summary of the thesis and main points go here

B. The challenge to the reader goes here if this is a persuasive essay

C. The memento or closing statement goes here

Common Mistakes

We've already looked at many common problems and mistakes that students make when they write. There are a few more that we should look at before you start writing.

Plurals

One of the most common errors that students make when writing is not using enough plurals. There seem to be two different problems going on here. First, students forget to add an "S" to the noun when used with counting words, like numbers, and words like "many", "most", and "some". But on the other hand, students seem to rarely use plurals when discussing preferences or categories or non-specific nouns.

Counting words and Plural Nouns

✗	There are many reason for this opinion.	✓	There are many reasons for this opinion.
✗	We ate some apple yesterday.*	✓	We ate some apples yesterday.
✗	Five student were absent.	✓	Five students were absent.
✗	There are lots of problem with the plan.	✓	There are lots of problems with the plan.

* "Some apple" might be right in some situations. If "some" means 1 specific but not important apple, then the sentence is correct. On the other hand, if "some" means "a few apples", then it is wrong.

Preferences/Categories/Non-specific Nouns

✗	I really like bagel for breakfast.	✓	I really like bagels for breakfast.
✗	Student at Soongsil need more facility.	✓	Students at Soongsil need more facilities.
✗	Grizzly bear is very dangerous.	✓	Grizzly bears are very dangerous.
✗	Another university has larger campus.	✓	Other universities have larger campuses.
✗	We usually sing a song after drinking.	✓	We usually sing songs after drinking.

Comma/Capitalization

Another problem that seems to come up in almost every assignment is the capitalization after a comma mistake. After a comma, you cannot capitalize the next UNLESS it is a proper, named noun. There are no exceptions.

✗	However, It is often busy on Saturdays.
✗	According to the Chosun Ilbo, Student loans have an average interest rate of 5.6%
✗	In conclusion, We should study at least ten minutes every day to not forget what we've learned.
✗	Secondly, Add salt and pepper to the pot.
✗	While Suji was studying in England, She made many great friends.

✓	However, it is often busy on Saturdays.
✓	According to the Chosun Ilbo, student loans have an average interest rate of 5.6%
✓	In conclusion, we should study at least ten minutes every day to not forget what we've learned.
✓	Secondly, add salt and pepper to the pot.
✓	While Suji was studying in England, she made many great friends.

Modals

Modals refer to special auxiliary (helper) verbs that help express conditional propositions, how the world should be or might be. Modals include *can, could, should, would, may, must, and might.* Other verbs play a similar role: *have to, ought to, need to.*

When writing persuasive essays, these modals are very important because they let the author talk about the world in the way she wants it to be, if her opinion is accepted.

Should = it would be a good idea to do / it is the right thing to do

Have to/Must = it is required (no choice) to do

Ought to = it is proper/right to do

Need to = it is necessary to do

Can = it is possible to do

Could = if things were/become different it was/is possible to do; also: past possibilities, polite requests

Would = if things were different, it will have been done / in the past it will have been done but not now / polite, soft request

Might = there is a chance that it will be done

May = it is permitted to do/there is a chance that it will be done

The three hardest modals for students are *should, could*, and *would.*

Examples

- *Do you think I should tell the professor that I will be absent tomorrow?*
  → *Do you think it is a good idea for me to tell the professor that I will be absent tomorrow?*
- *We should hurry if we want to eat before the movie.*
  → *It is a good idea for us to hurry if we want to eat before the movie.*
- *Women should be paid the same salary as men.*
  → *It is the right thing to do for women to be paid as much as men.*

Could

- *If you had called me, I could have met you at the station.*
  → *If you had called me, it may have been possible to have met you at the station.*
- *When they were young, they could drink water directly from the stream.*
  → *When they were young, it was possible to drink water directly from the stream but now they can't.*
- *Could you hand me a tissue?*
  → *Is it possible for you to hand me a tissue?*
- *If the government passes this law, it could have a major impact.*
  → *If the government passes this law, it is possible that it might have a major impact.*

Would

- *If it hadn't rained, we would have been on time.*
  → *If it hadn't rained, we could have had the ability to be on time.*
- *What would you do if you were me?*
  → *What action might you take if you were me?*
- *It would be good for students and their families if tuition were lower.*
  → *Things could be better for students and their families if tuition were lower.*

Exercises

Exercise 15.1

Fill in the outline for the essay.

Dogs Versus Cats

Do you have a pet? If so, what kind is it? If not, what kind would you want? Personally, I have a dog and a cat, but I think dogs are the best kind of pet. There are several reasons for this opinion.

First, dogs are more fun. They love to run around and chase things. You can throw a stick or ball and a dog will run after it and bring it back to you. Have you ever tried that with a cat? A cat might chase the ball, but good luck getting it back. Cats are best at catching mice, but overall dogs are more exciting. Dogs are much more playful and are more energetic playmates.

Secondly, dogs are smarter, usually. Animal trainers agree, dogs are easier to train than cats. Also, dogs can remember more commands and can understand more commands. They learn faster than cats, too. Cats can learn some tricks and commands, but most breeds of dog are more intelligent.

Finally, dogs are more loving. Dogs come from wolves and wolves live in large packs, so dogs are more familiar with living in groups. Cats are loners, so cats are the best at living on their own. Dogs are more sociable; they need others around them. When I come home, my dog is more excited to see me. My cat only cares about me if I have some food for her.

So, I think dogs are the best pets. Cats are best at some things, but dogs are better companions. Dogs are better friends than cats. If you are looking for a pet that will love you, get a dog.

I. Introduction

1. (hook) ________________

2. (thesis) ________________

3. (preview)

A. ________________

B. ________________

C. ________________

II. Body

1. Dogs more fun

A. ________________

B. ________________

C. Cats chase mice; dogs more exciting

2. Dogs smarter

A. Animal trainers: dogs easier to train

B. ________________

C. ________________

3. Dogs more loving

A. ________________

B. Cats = loners, can live alone

C. ________________

III. Conclusion

1. (summary) ________________

2. cats okay, dogs better

3. (memento) ________________

Exercises

Exercise 15.2

Correct the words that should be plurals, not singular.

1. Many student work part-time job.
2. These day, our nation has several problem.
3. She collects doll and old book.
4. In fall, I love to eat mandarin orange from Jeju Island.
5. If I had a lot of money, I'd buy a few thing for my family.

Exercise 15.3

Fill in the sentences with *should*, *would*, or *could*.

1. I think we _______ leave soon, before the snow storm gets here.
2. If I were you, I _______ ask my professor for some more time.
3. Many people thought the government _______ respond to the problem sooner.
4. It was believed that cockroaches _______ survive a nuclear bomb blast, but that is mostly not true.
5. There _______ be more options for eating at the university.

Memo

Unit 16 Are You Ready to Write?

Objectives

- Reviewing the writing process

Step 1 Pre-writing

This step is too often forgotten by students as they rush to do their assignment. But, if you ask successful students and professional writers, you will find that they never skip the pre-writing step. There are four main things to do in the pre-writing stage: determine the subject, brainstorm ideas, narrow our focus, and make notes.

- [ ] Determine the subject
- [ ] Brainstorm ideas
- [ ] Narrow the focus
- [ ] Make notes

To determine the subject, you usually just need to get the assignment from your instructor, since most essays you will write are for school. In some cases, though, you have a more broad assignment, just write an essay. Let's say that your instructor says "Write an essay about a current social issue."

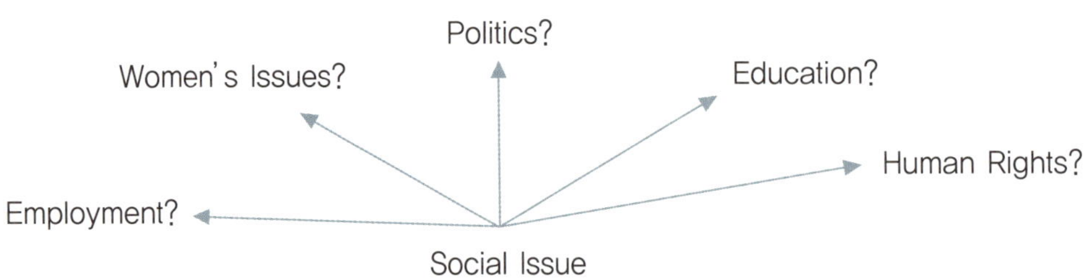

As you can see, "social issues" is a broad category of subjects. To write a good essay, you will definitely have to narrow your focus to something much smaller and more specific. You could brainstorm some ideas from "social issues", or if you can think of something more specific already, you could pick that. For our lesson, let's go with Education.

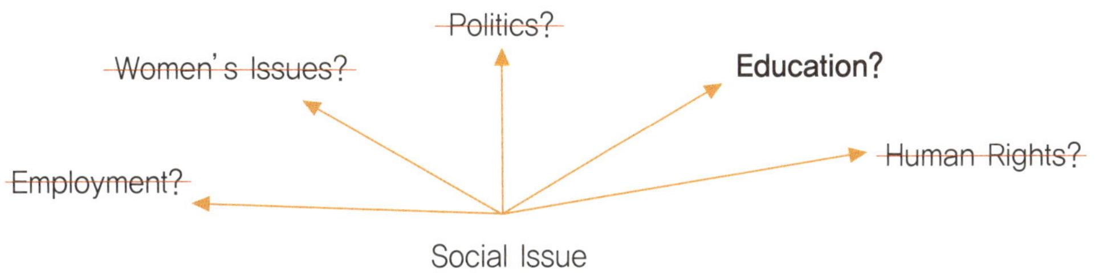

Now that you have your more specific subject – education – it's time to build up some ideas. That's where brainstorming comes in. There are many ways to come up with ideas. You could just make a list of things related to the subject. You can use one of the various methods of mind-mapping. For our lesson, we'll use the traditional brainstorm.

Start by drawing a circle in the middle of a blank paper and writing the subject in the middle. Then, set a time limit, maybe 10 or 15 minutes, and write down every idea you have about the topic, no matter how silly, stupid, or strange the idea might be.

✓ Determine the subject

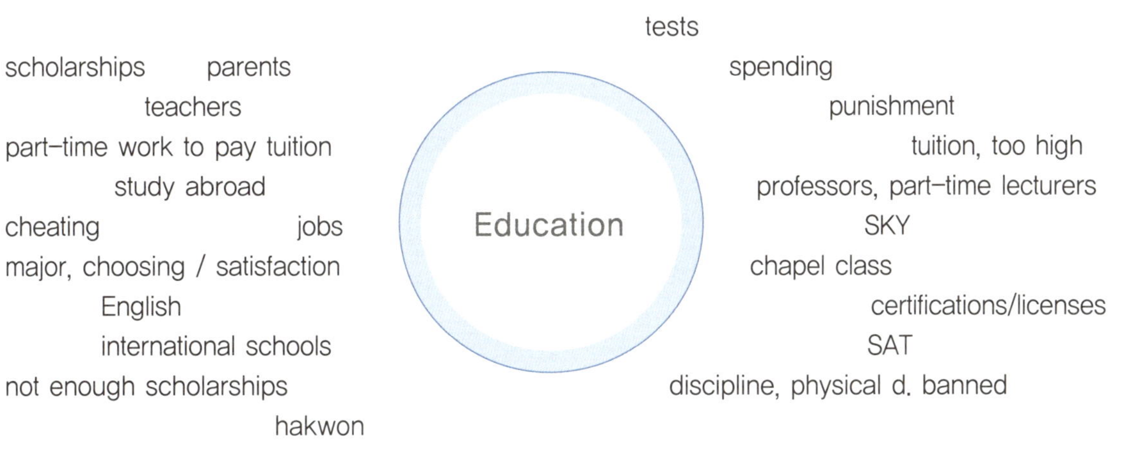

From our example, we can see that there are many possible sets of choices for an essay about education. Several of them could make a good essay. You could write about the ban on physical punishment in the classroom. You could write about the SKY system and how it affects society. You might want to write about whether getting licenses and certificates is a good way to get a job. While all of these are good choices, we are going to pick tuition and educational spending for our lesson. Now that we have narrowed our focus, we should take some notes and do a little research. If there is material related to your topic in your course's textbook, start there and make notes about important pages, charts and graphs, and so on. Also, you should check the internet and look for articles, reports, studies, research, and other information about the subject you've chosen.

- [x] Brainstorm ideas
- [x] Narrow the focus
- [x] Make notes

Step 2 Planning

You've finished the pre-writing stage, so it's time to get started with Planning. Like the last stage, there are a few parts to Planning. The work you did in the previous step should have given you plenty of things to think about, so now it's time to form an opinion about the topic. In general, and especially for persuasive essay, the thesis statement reflects the author's opinion about the topic. If you need a review of writing thesis statements, go back to the unit on introductions and look through the material again. In our case, there are a few possibilities, but one idea seems clearly more important and interesting.

- [ ] Write thesis statement
- [ ] Finish research
- [ ] Make an outline

Thesis: "In my opinion, universities and the government must do more to lower the cost of education."

- [x] Write thesis statement

Having written our thesis statement, we should now check our notes and make sure we have all the data and information we need. This may mean that you will need to do some more research, read some more articles, and make more notes. The idea here is to have everything you need to write before you start writing the essay itself. When you feel like you have all the information you need, you can move to the next part.

✓ Finish research

Now comes a really important part: the outline. This is another step many students try to skip, but if you skip it, you will almost always get a worse grade. In the spring semester, we said an outline for an essay was the same as blueprints for building a house, and for good reason. The outline helps you decide what information to use and what order to put the information in. Taking the time to make an outline will be worth it when you write your essay.

We've already seen some outline's in the past few units, and you probably remember the outlines we looked at last semester. In case you don't remember well, though, we'll walk through another one now.

First, we add a Roman number for each of the main sections. I, one or /eye/, is for the introduction, and V, five or /vee/, is for the conclusion. Some people like the make the essay's body II and the conclusion III. Others prefer to make one Roman numeral for each main point. Either way is okay. For our example, we'll use one Roman numeral for each main point.

Let's start with the introduction. As you remember from earlier, the introduction has three parts: the hook, the thesis statement, and the preview. We already have the thesis statement.

We need a hook and the preview. To do the hook, we should think about something that would be interesting to the audience and related to the topic. If you need to review hooks, check out unit four again. Remember, when we write a hook, it's important to remember who the readers are; that will help you figure out what would be interesting to them. In our case, we can assume the readers are other university students, so perhaps an anecdote – a personal story – would be a good choice for a hook. For this essay about the high cost of university fees, a story about having to work part time to pay for the tuition and maybe getting bad grades or having to take a year off of school to pay for the next year, these could be good.

Now we need to do the preview. Looking back at our brainstorming and the research we've done, we can figure out three main supporting details: starts students off with a big disadvantage; there is no added value for the higher cost; heavy burden on families. But, just knowing the three main points isn't enough; we also need to know what order to put them in for the strongest impact. This is sometimes obvious and sometimes just your personal taste. In this case, none of the three are obviously particularly stronger, so we have to decide which matters the most to us and put it last. For our example essay, we want to spend several sentences talking about how having loans or getting lower grades or taking longer to finish school gives students, especially male students, a big negative when they start looking for work later and through several years of their life. So, since that will be the longest paragraph in the body, we'll put it third, using the "strongest last" strategy.

From there we will do the body and the conclusion in a similar way. To save time, we'll fill in everything. If you need more practice with the body and conclusion, please repeat units five and six.

I. introduction

A. part time job, getting bad grades because always tired

B. In my opinion, universities and the government must do more to lower the cost of tuition.

C. The preview

1. Heavy burden on family
2. No added value for higher costs
3. students start with big disadvantage

II. Heavy burden on family

A. Global economic trouble

1. Incomes lower or not growing
2. Prices higher for everything
    i. Food *(Economics Report, November 2010)*
    ii. Clothing *(Joongang Ilbo, December12th, 2010)*

B. Many education costs

1. Hakwons
    i. average family spends 1,000,000 won/month (Chosunllbo, June13th, 2010)
2. Tutors
3. University
    i. Average cost 6.84 million won / year (http://www.tradingmarkets.com, April 2010)

III. No added value for higher costs

A. Classrooms not improved

1. electronic whiteboards
2. more computers

B. Universities use part-time lecturers, not full professors

1. (www.koreabrand.net, Oct 30, 2010)

C. Class sizes too large

1. my class average, 42 students

IV. Students start with big disadvantage

A. Debt

1. student loans
    i. can accumulate 25 million won or more in debt for university
    ii. burden on student and family
    iii. delay buying house or car, starting family

B. Lost time

1. part-time work, less time

i. no club activities

ii. no time for licenses or certificates

2. military service, men lose two years already
3. gap years for earning tuition
4. rich students have more opportunities.

V. Conclusion.

A. summary

B. (challenge) email to National Assembly and university president, join demonstrations, tell friends

C. (memento) save our students, save our country

☑ Make an outline

Step 3 Drafting

Now that the outline is done, it's time to write the first draft. Take your outline and turn the keywords, phrases and notes into a five – or more – paragraph essay. Let's take our example outline and write an essay.

The Social Costs of High Tuition

I was very excited to start university. But, when I saw how much the tuition was, my excitement disappeared. My parents couldn't afford to pay all of it since my older sister was already in university. There are very few scholarships, so I couldn't count on getting any assistance from that. The only way to pay for my school fees was to get a part time job. My story is not unique; thousands of students have to work to pay for school. In my opinion, universities and the government must do more to lower university tuition. There are three reasons for my opinion. First, the high cost puts a heavy burden on families. Secondly, there is no value that we can see from the high costs. Finally, it puts students at a big disadvantage.

First, the always increasing price of university tuition has a heavy impact on families. With the global recession, families are already struggling to pay for the basics, like food and clothing which have risen in price by nearly twenty percent and over fifteen percent since 2008, respectively (Economics Report, November 2010; Joongang Ilbo, December 12th, 2010). Of course, Korean families are famous for paying a lot for their children's education. The average family in Seoul spends about one million won a month per child on hakwons and tutors (Chosun Ilbo, June 13th, 2010). If a family has more than one child, those costs grow much heavier. Yet, to succeed in Korea's competitive job market, families must invest in their children's future very early. Thus, when it comes time to pay for university tuition, which averages over six million a year, many families just cannot afford the cost (www.tradingmarkets.com).

Secondly, there is little value given to students for these high costs. If students feeled like the higher costs of university tuition were giving them more advantages, then it would not feel so bad. As it is, most universitys try to hire lots of part-time lectures instead of full-time professors (www.koreabrand.net). My economics professor is a part-time lecturer; she is very good but doesn't earn very much for her teaching. Class sizes is too large; In my case, the averige class size is 42 student. In talking with my friends at other schools, I found that this is common. Furthermore, Classrooms are not keeping up with technology A few universities use electronic white boards, but most do not. Electronic white boards are very cutting edge technology. Moreover, most classroom don't even have a computer; If the lecturer needs to show a presentation or video, they have to bring they're own's notebook computer.

Finally, these high costs give many students a big disadvantage. For example, many families take out a student loan to pay the tuition. This debt, which can be more than 25 million won in many cases, means that a graduate will start his or her working life with a giant stone tied around his neck. Instead of buying a car or a house and starting a family, they have to pay for the loan for many years. On the other hand, students who choose to work instead of taking out loans are also at a disadvantage. Instead of studying diligently, earning certificates and licenses, and doing useful club activities, they are working at coffee shops and restaurants. The problem is even worse for men because they already lose so much time in the military. These problems affect students from poor and middle class families more than rich families, creating a greater social and economic divide in the country.

So, in conclusion, I believe that universities and the government need to help us by lowering tuition because it is hurting families and graduates' futures and doesn't improve the quality of education. There are many things you can do to help spread this message. Email the members of the National Assembly and the president of the university. Tell your friends to do that too. Join other students at protests and demonstrations. If we all work together, we can save our futures and save our country, too.

Steps 4 & 5 Editing & Revising

So now that the essay's first draft is finished, you will need to find all the mistakes and problems – Step 4 – and then fix them – Step 5. Look at this check list for some ideas of what to look for when you edit.

	Structural Edits		Logical Edits
□	All sentences end with . ! ?	□	The thesis is strong and easy to understand.
□	All sentences have a subject and verb; subject-verb agreement (I go, she goes)	□	The introduction has an interesting hook that relates to the reader.
□	The first word of every sentence, proper names, and abbreviations are capitalized. Check for problems with I, it, if, in, and is.	□	The introduction gives a preview of the main ideas in the essay, and in the same order that they appear.
□	Each new paragraph is indented.	□	The rule of three or another structural pattern (cause/effect, problem/solution) is used to for supporting details.
□	There are no fragments or clauses without sentences. Check any sentence that starts with Because, Since, or So to be certain.	□	Each of the paragraphs supports the thesis.
□	Plural nouns are used when referring to general things. (I like kittens. Students need to study.)	□	In each paragraph, there is no extra or unrelated information.
□	*They're, their, there* are all used correctly.	□	Facts, statistics, and other factual data have the source listed (According to the *Oxford International Dictionary*…)
□	*For example, for instance, like*, and *such as* are used correctly.	□	The supporting ideas are arranged in the strongest order (strongest last, chronological, etc).
□	Adjectives and nouns are not confused. (She has an ~~activity~~ active personality.)	□	The conclusion has a summary of the thesis and main ideas.
□	Pronouns are used instead of repeating nouns. (The monkey is in the tree. It is very cute.)	□	The conclusion has a strong closing statement (memento).

Secondly, there is little value given to students for these high costs. If students feeled like the higher costs of university tuition were giving them more advantages, then it would not feel so bad. As it is, most universitys try to hire lots of part-time lectures instead of full-time professors (www.koreabrand.net). My economics professor is a part-time lecturer; she is very good but doesn't earn very much for her teaching. Class sizes is too large; In my case, the averige class size is 42 student. In talking with my friends at other schools, I found that this is common. Furthermore, Classrooms are not keeping up with technology A few universities use electronic white boards, but most do not. Electronic white boards are very cutting edge technology. Moreover, most classroom don't even have a computer; If the lecturer needs to show a presentation or video, they have to bring they're own's notebook computer.

Take a moment and see how many mistakes you can find. How many did you find? Hold your mouse over the highlighted parts to see the reason why they are wrong. After you've read the essay several times and found as many problems as possible, it is time to rewrite it and fix all the mistakes. The goal is to improve the essay as much as possible in the next draft of it.

Secondly, there is little value given to students for these high costs. If students feeled like the higher costs of university tuition were giving them more advantages, then it would not feel so bad. As it is, most universitys try to hire lots of part-time lectures instead of full-time professors (www.koreabrand.net). My economics professor is a part-time lecturer; she is very good but doesn't earn very much for her teaching. Class sizes is too large; In my case, the averige class size is 42 student. In talking with my friends at other schools, I found that this is common. Furthermore, Classrooms are not keeping up with technology A few universities use electronic white boards, but most do not. Electronic white boards are very cutting edge technology. Moreover, most classroom don't even have a computer; If the lecturer needs to show a presentation or video, they have to bring they're own's notebook computer.

Tip try to wait several hours or a couple of days before editing so that your mind is clear and fresh.

Secondly, there is little value given to students for these high costs. If students ~~feeled~~ felt like the higher costs of university tuition were giving them more advantages, then it would not feel so bad. As it is, most ~~universitys~~ universities try to hire lots of part-time lecturers instead of full-time professors (www.koreabrand.net). ~~My economics professor is a part-time lecturer; she is very good but doesn't earn very much for her teaching.~~ Class sizes ~~is~~ are too large; ~~In~~ in my case, the averige ~~average~~ class size is 42 ~~student~~ students. In talking with my friends at other schools, I found that this is common. Furthermore, ~~Classrooms~~ classrooms are not keeping up with technology. A few universities use electronic white boards, but most do not. ~~Electronic white boards are very cutting edge technology.~~ Moreover, most classroom don't even have a computer; ~~If~~ if the lecturer needs to show a presentation or video, they have to bring ~~they're~~ their ~~own's~~ own notebook computer.

After you finish rewriting the first draft, you need to edit the 2nd draft again and then rewrite it too. Keep editing and rewriting until it's perfect.

Exercises

Exercise 16.1

Read the paragraph and then fill in the with the correct information. Do not use full sentences on the outline.

The Deadly Cell

Every year 380,000 people, mostly children, die from something preventable: *e.coli* infections. By understanding how *e.coli* is spread, we can reduce the number of deaths caused by these bacteria. The main ways that *e.coli* is spread are: unclean food preparation, unsanitary farm conditions, and contaminated water supplies. Each method is preventable with proper education and training, access to reliable farm supplies, and money for water facilities. There are many organizations that are working on these issues around the world. Please help the fight by contributing your time and money. Your efforts will save lives!

I. Introduction

A. (hook) ______________________________

B. (topic sentence) ______________________________

II. Body

A. (detail 1) ______________________________

B. (detail 2) ______________________________

C. (detail 3) ______________________________

III. Conclusion

A. (challenge) ______________________________

B. (memento) ______________________________

Exercise 16.2

Rewrite the essay below, correcting the mechanical and formatting mistakes.

When you look at the night sky, Do you wonder if there is anyone up there.
Since ancient times, people have look to the sky for answer to that question.
The scientists at SETI is very concerned with that question. in this essay we will look at who SETI is, how they look for alien live, and learn about their most intriguing discovery
First, SETI stands for the Search for Extra-Terrestrial Intelligence. SETI is not one specific group of persons, however. There is many activity around the world through various university and private research facilities that contribute to the search for alien.
While some experiments were performed as early as 1896, SETI as we know It today began in 1960 at Cornell University by astronomer Frank Drake. Today, thousands of astronomers, hobbyists, and others spends at least part of their time looking for alien life.
Secondly, let us look at how SETI works?
Using giant telescopes around the World, they search through the vast amount of space look for signs from intelligent civilizations on distant planet. There are 8 planets in our solar system and several dwarf planets like Pluto and Sedna.
Various projects at large telescopes and university around the world use radio signals and other data to look for signs of intelligent civilizations on other planet. In the early years, getting enough equipment to searching for these signs was a problem. By contrast, today there is too much data to examine easily, So a innovative computer program called SETI@home was developing.
Anyone can downloads this software which uses they's computer whenever its not busy. Through this method, billions of mathematical calculations can be perform with little effort.
Finally, has SETI found any proof of alien life!
Actually, thus far, no definite proof of life on another planets have been finded.
In 1977, though, A mysterious radio signal was discovered by a seti researcher in ohio.

The signal seemed like it might be from a intelligent civilization. The researcher was so surprised, he writed "Wow!" on the printout.
unfortunately the Wow signal was never repeated, So scientists could not confirm it!
As you can see, SETI is an interesting set of projects and study that looks for signs of intelligent life on other world While no proof of aliens have been seen yet, they's efforts have helped to innovate many technologies for space exploration. Maybe someday we will found another Wow signal from someone, somewhere in the universe.

Essay Assessment

Use these pages to help prepare for your paragraph assessment.
Your instructor should provide you with a topic for the essay.

Follow these steps as you start working on your essay.

Step 1 Pre-writing

- ☐ Get topic from instructor
- ☐ Brainstorm ideas about topic
- ☐ Narrow your focus

Step 2 Planning

- ☐ Write a thesis sentence
- ☐ Create a brain map
- ☐ Complete an outline

Step 3 Drafting

- ☐ Write the first (rough) draft

Step 4 Editing

- ☐ Don't look at the essay for at least one day
- ☐ Read the essay carefully
- ☐ Mark any mistakes, typos, or problems; make notes as you read

Step 5 Revising

- ☐ Fix the mistakes from Step four
- ☐ Write next draft of the essay
- ☐ Repeat Steps four and five until you have a perfect draft

Step 1 Brainstorm

Topic (from instructor): ____

Step 1 Narrow Your Focus

Look again at the ideas you wrote on the brainstorm page. Group similar ideas together and write them here. You may not need all the groups or lines.

Group 1

Group 2

Group 3

Group 4

Other ideas that don't fit in groups:

Step 2 Write a Thesis Statement

Topic (from instructor): ______________________________

Review the topic from the instructor and read through your brainstorming and focus notes. Based on these factors, write a thesis statement that will guide your entire essay. Generally, thesis statement are your opinion about the subject. In many cases, you should be able to write "In my opinion..." in front of your thesis statement.

Examples

In my opinion, we must do more to stop global warming.
(In my opinion) Google will be the most powerful technology company in the world soon.
I believe that respect is the most important aspect of a healthy marriage.
(I believe that) Practice with native speakers is the only way to really learn a language.

Thesis Statement: (In my opinion)

____

Three supporting details:

Detail 1 ______________________________

Detail 2 ______________________________

Detail 3 ______________________________

Step 2 Create a mind Map

Use this page to help visualize your essay.

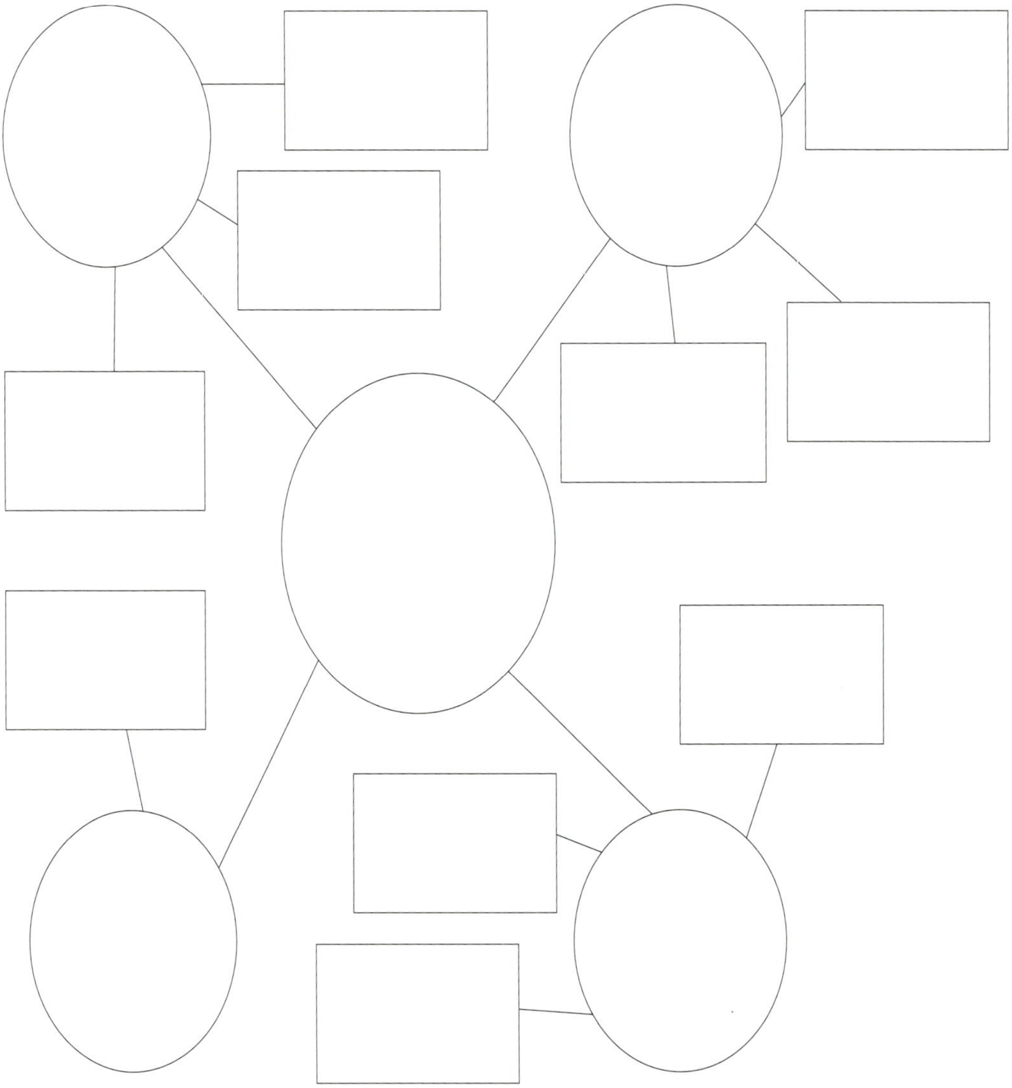

Step 2 Complete an Outline

Use the following pages to create your outline. Remember, you do not need to write complete sentences on the outline; key words and phrases, facts and figures are sufficient. You should, however, write your thesis statement and any direct quotes from other people in full sentence form.

There are many lines for details and sub-details. You may not need all of them.

Use only those that you need.

I. Introduction

- A. (hook)____________________
    1. ____________________
    2. ____________________
- B. (thesis statement) ____________________
- C. Preview
    1. (detail 1)____________________
    2. (detail 2)____________________
    3. (detail 3)____________________

II. (Detail 1) ____________________

- A. ____________________
    1. ____________________
    2. ____________________
- B. ____________________
    1. ____________________
    2. ____________________
- C. ____________________
    1. ____________________
    2. ____________________

III. (Detail 2) ____________________

- A. ____________________
    1. ____________________
    2. ____________________

B. ______________________________

1. ____

2. ____

C. ______________________________

1. ____

2. ____

IV. (Detail 3) _________________________

A. ______________________________

1. ____

2. ____

B. ______________________________

1. ____

2. ____

C. ______________________________

1. ____

2. ____

V. Conclusion

A. (summary)_________________________

B. (challenge)_________________________

C. (memento)_________________________

Additional notes for the essay

Essay – first draft

In the space below, write the first draft of the paragraph you have been planning on the previous pages. Do not worry about making mistakes. The first draft does not need to be perfect. Focus on developing the ideas and support for your topic sentence.

________________ (title)

Step four – editing

Now you will read through your essay and look for mistakes.
Use the checklist below to help you with this process.

	Structural Edits		Logical Edits
☐	All sentences end with . ! ?	☐	The thesis is strong and easy to understand.
☐	All sentences have a subject and verb; subject-verb agreement (I go, she goes)	☐	The introduction has an interesting hook that relates to the reader.
☐	The first word of every sentence, proper names, and abbreviations are capitalized. Check for problems with *I*, *it*, *if*, *in*, and *is*.	☐	The introduction gives a preview of the main ideas in the essay, and in the same order that they appear.
☐	Each new paragraph is indented.	☐	The rule of three or another structural pattern (cause/effect, problem/solution) is used to for supporting details.
☐	There are no fragments or clauses without sentences. Check any sentence that starts with *Because*, *Since*, or *So* to be certain.	☐	Each of the paragraphs supports the thesis.
☐	Plural nouns are used when referring to general things. (I like kittens. Students need to study.)	☐	In each paragraph, there is no extra or unrelated information.
☐	*They're*, *their*, *there* are all used correctly.	☐	Facts, statistics, and other factual data have the source listed (According to *the Oxford International Dictionary*…)
☐	*For example*, *for instance*, *like*, and *such as* are used correctly.	☐	The supporting ideas are arranged in the strongest order (strongest last, chronological, etc).
☐	Adjectives and nouns are not confused. *(She has an activity ~~active~~ personality.)*	☐	The conclusion has a summary of the thesis and main ideas.
☐	Pronouns are used instead of repeating nouns. (The monkey is in the tree ~~The monkey~~ It is very cute.)	☐	The conclusion has a strong closing statement (memento).

Step five – revising | second draft

Using the list of problems you discovered in step four, rewrite your essay. This second draft should be much better than the first draft.

Repeat step four with this second draft. When you have read it several times and can find no more mistakes, write or type the final draft and give it to your instructor.

Name__________ Number__________

Memo

Answer Key

Foundation of Freshman English Writing

Answer Key

Unit 01 What Are Paragraphs?

Exercise 1.1

1) On Wednesday, Dami and Wonhee ate some Italian food.
2) The cat watched us as we sat in the park.
3) Did you see the movie?
4) Cecilia is my sister.
5) The computer crashes every time I open this program.
6) In my opinion, *Winnie the Pooh* is the best children's story.
7) Yesterday was Tuesday, wasn't it?
8) According to the news, it might rain tomorrow.
9) Jincheol's skiing trip will be delayed until next week.
10) When he was young, he lived in the Philippines.

Exercise 1.2

Who is your hero – For me, it's my grandfather. He is the bravest and smartest person I know. He left a farm in a rural Kansas to join the US Army after he Japanese attacked Pearl Harbor. He won several medals for his brave actions. After the war, he started a business in the new field of computer programming and though he did not become rich, he was able to give a good life to his children. I hope I can follow in his footsteps.

Exercise 1.3

There are six rules or guidelines for writing proper paragraphs. The first sentence should be indented several spaces to the right. If you are typing on a website, though, you can use a blank line. Secondly, all the sentences should follow proper grammar rules. This means that the first word and proper names should be capitalized, ending punctuation must be used, the subject and predicate verb must agree with each other, and there should be no fragments or run-on sentences. Next, a paragraph has only one main idea and every sentence should support that idea. If you want to talk about a different topic, you should start a new paragraph. Finally, make sure all the sentences follow each other; do not put each sentence on its own line. That's a poem, not a paragraph! If you pay attention to these rules, you will be writing good paragraphs in no time.

Exercise 1.4

1. This is my cousin Robert from Sydney.
2. On Monday, October twentieth we're going to see *Les Miserables.*
3. Luxury products like, Prada and Gucci, from America and Europe can be very expensive in Korea.
4. Wonbin was having problems with Microsoft Word, so he didn't finish Professor Kim's homework assignment.
5. Manchester United beat Chelsea two goals to one in the game on Friday.
6. Next Wednesday, I am going to Busan by KTX.
7. When I saw Haesun on Christmas day, she said her father was in the hospital.
8. If you want to go to Harvard University, you'll have to speak English really well.
9. After the end of the Vietnam War, the Vietnamese government changed the name of Saigon to Ho Chi Min City.
10. As the H.M.S. Titanic was sinking in the Atlantic Ocean, the crew sent out an S.O.S. signal.

Exercise 1.5

1. ?
2. ! !
3. .
4. ?
5. .
6. ! !
7. ?
8. !
9. .
10. ?

Exercise 1.6

1. Chang <u>sees</u> a new movie every week
2. They <u>always</u> eat at restaurants, never at home.
3. Yale <u>is</u> a major university in the United States.
4. A simple notebook computer <u>costs</u> about $600.
5. Keith likes Mary, so he <u>is going to ask</u> her for a date this weekend.
6. There <u>are</u> many problems with this design.
7. The professor and her students <u>are</u> in the computer lab.
8. I <u>am</u> going to the cafeteria, do you want to come?
9. We <u>get</u> lots of rain during the monsoon.
10. Korea <u>has</u> four distinct seasons.

Exercise 1.7

1. X
2. X
3. O
4. X
5. X
6. O
7. X
8. X
9. O
10. X

Exercise 1.8

Different cultures have different ideas about time. In some countries, it is very important to be on time. Being late will make people angry. People in these countries like to do one task, complete it, and the move to the next. In other countries, however, people are more relaxed about time. Being late is not a problem. People often have different appointments at the same time and do many different activities together.

Unit 02 What Are Paragraphs?

Exercise 2.1

1. D
2. P
3. D
4. P
5. P
6. D
7. D
8. P
9. D
10. D

Exercise 2.2

1. Persuasive
2. Descriptive

Exercise 2.3

1. Toys were so much better when I was a child. .... Children today just don't have the great toys I did.
2. Web page functionality has improved dramatically since the Internet was created. ... As connection speeds increase, web pages will only become more exciting.

Exercise 2.4

These are suggestions; there are many right answers.

1. We can make our neighborhood beautiful again. / There are many things we can do to clean up our neighborhood
2. There are several things to consider when buying a new laptop.
3. I learned many things when my pet cat Mittens died.

Exercise 2.5

F	F	O	O	F	O
O	F	F	O	F	F
O	O	F	O	O	F
O	O	O	F	F	F

Unit 03 The Foundation: Sentence Structure

Exercise 3.1

These answers are suggestions. There are many right answers.

Q. What do Jamie, Kevin, and Mark do on the weekend?
A. They watch movies on the weekend.
Q. What does a diligent student do every week?
A. She goes to the library.
Q. What does Mina do all the time?
A. She goes shopping all the time.
Q. What does Daniel do on Wednesdays?
A. He plays tennis.
Q. What do students do every day?
A. They study.

Exercise 3.2

1. Jinhee studies English for two hours a day.
2. Claire and Tony watch movies on the weekend.
3. The cat sits in the sun every afternoon.
4. The teacher prepares for class in the evening.
5. Ghosts live in the old house.
6. On Saturday, I usually walk in the park.
7. According to this article, black and white will be fashionable this year
8. Prof. Nam sends email everyday.
9. At Christmas time, Americans buy lots of gifts for family and friends.
10. Johnny Depp's new movie is not very interesting.

Exercise 3.3

1. Some students were late.
2. The answer is wrong.
3. A mother and her baby were crossing the street.
4. Money and information are important in the global economy.
5. Tae-sub didn't do his homework.
6. Alicia and Ji-yeon weren't at the meeting.
7. Tomorrow the weather is going to be awful.
8. If you drink too much soju, you will be sick tomorrow.
9. The new teacher wants to learn all the students' names.
10. There is a table and lamp in the bedroom.

Exercise 3.4

1. A butterfly landed on the flower.
2. The teacher gave a lot of homework.
3. Stephanie missed her bus.
4. Can you hand me the book please?
5. If you are tired, drink some coffee.

Exercise 3.5

1. On Sunday, my family usually goes to church.
2. We're going to need clothes, a sleeping bag, food, and water for the camping trip.
3. Hey Jeongmin, did you hear that the test is cancelled?
4. My new address is 415 Maple Street, Peoria, Illinois, 61064.
5. "Let's go," said Sarah to her friends.

6. Last Friday, Julie met Michael, Henry, Sarah, and Katie at the Hyatt Hotel.
7. Professor Steven Jones married Doctor Izumi Saito in Vancouver, British Columbia, Canada on August 15th, 2007.
8. I was studying for Prof. Choi's long, difficult Chinese exam when my mother, Veronica, called to tell me to stop by E-mart and buy cheese, cereal, lettuce, and onions.
9. So, if Margaret flies to K.L, Malaysia, she can save almost 300000 won.
10. On Monday, July 23rd, Dahyeon prepared an American-style barbecue with sausages, hamburgers, hot dogs, and potato salad.

Unit 04 The Ties That Bind: Unity & Transition

Exercise 4.1

A

Fair Trade Coffee

Do you like coffee? I do. I drink coffee every day. But recently I learned that many coffee shops buy their beans from large companies that do not support their workers well. In fact, many of these companies keep their costs low by using children to do the hardest work. ~~Children should be in school~~. Fair trade coffee comes directly from the coffee farmers; no large companies earn money from the farmers' work. ~~Farming is very difficult work for them.~~ Next time you want a cup of joe, please order fair trade coffee. It's the right thing to do.

B

Coco Chanel

If you walk down the street in Gangnam or Apgujeong, you will see many women, and some men, wearing clothes with a double C logo, the emblem for the famous luxury brand Chanel. But do you know who founded this iconic company? Chanel was created by French fashion designer Coco Chanel. She was born Gabreille Chanel in Saumur, France in 1883. ~~Gabreille was a common~~ girl's name. She learned how to make clothes when she was an orphan at age twelve. At 18, she left the orphanage and became a cabaret singer, using the name Coco. She soon fell in love with a rich textile factory owner and started making clothes in her own shops. From there, she became one of the most respected and influential fashion designers in the world. Her life is inspiring to many, rising from a poor orphan to the highest ranks of a glamorous industry. ~~The clothing is very high quality.~~

Exercise 4.2

Paragraph A.

Topic sentence: But recently I learned that many coffee shops buy their beans from large companies that do not support their workers well.

Supporting detail 1: In fact, many of these companies keep their costs low by using children to do the hardest work.

Supporting detail 2: That's why I now only buy fair trade coffee.

Supporting detail 3: Fair trade coffee comes directly from the coffee farmers; no large companies earn money from the farmers' work.

Paragraph B.

Topic sentence: Chanel was created by French fashion designer Coco Chanel.

Supporting detail 1: She was born Gabreille Chanel in Saumur, France in 1883.

Supporting detail 2: She learned how to make clothes when she was an orphan at age twelve.

Supporting detail 3: At 18, she left the orphanage and became a cabaret singer, using the name Coco.

Supporting detail 4: She soon fell in love with a rich textile factory owner and started making clothes in her own shops.

Exercise 4.3

Topic sentence: While bears are important to Korea's culture, today they are in great danger.

Supporting detail 1: The moon bear, which has a white V shape on its chest, is very popular in traditional Chinese medicine.

Supporting detail 2: Because of this, some farmers keep moon bears in tiny cages and drain the liquid in their gallbladders(쓸개) to sell mostly to oriental medicine doctors in China and elsewhere.

Supporting detail 3: There are very few of these beautiful bears living in Jiri-san, so we must rescue the bears in farms to save the species.

Exercise 4.4

1. I talked to Sarah yesterday. She said that the test was really difficult.
2. Opium was one of the most important trade goods in the 1800s. Today it is a component of organized crime and terrorism.
3. One of the first popular reality TV shows was COPS. It showed real police officers fighting crime in a different city each week.
4. In my opinion, global warming is the most serious problem facing the world today. It affects everything from food to war and may soon kill millions of people.
5. Michael used to play basketball when he was in high school. In university though, he doesn't play it because he has a part-time job.
6. Yoko Ono is often seen as the person who destroyed the Beatles. However, she deserves credit as an influential artist.

7. Yesterday was very cold. It was also the first day of spring.
8. Some people think that the Great Wall of China is Asia's most important landmark. I think, however, that is not as impressive as Angkor Wat.
9. Ji-eun made spaghetti for lunch. However, she said it was not great.
10. Green tea is a traditional drink in Asia. Recently, however, it has also become popular in the West because it has many health benefits.

Unit 05 The Writing Process

Exercise 5.1

4 Editing
3 Drafting
1 Pre-writing
2 Planning
5 Revising

Exercise5.2

drafting In this step, you write the first, rough draft of the paragraph.
revising Now you will fix the problems you found in the previous step.
pre-writing Brainstorm ideas for the subject.
planning In this step, you will write the topic sentence and prepare an outline.
editing Look for mistakes such as misspellings and grammar problems.

Exercise 5.3

There are no correct answers; check that your answers fit each category.

Exercise 5.4

There are other ways to organize the ideas. These are suggestions.

Group 1	TV Stars	Group 2	programs
	Kim Joon		dramas
	Yoon Eun-hye		police dramas

Kim So-eun
Goo Hye-sun
Lee Min-ho
Song Ji-hyo

Group 3 Korean TV
Love Story in Praha
Boys Over Flowers
Winter Sonata

Educational shows
game shows
reality TV
sitcoms

Group 4 American shows
Friends
Sex and the City
CSI

Exercise 5.5

These are suggestions. Your answers may be different.

Group 1 There are many talented stars in Korean dramas.
Group 2 Modern television includes many different kinds of TV programs.
Group 3 Korean dramas offer an interesting view of Korean culture.
Group 4 American television shows have had a large impact around the world.

Exercise 5.6

A. IV
B. VII
C. X
D. II
E. XIII
F. L
G. LXIII
H. C
I. IXXX
J. CCIVXVI

Exercise 5.7

I
A
1
2
i
ii
B
1
i
ii
iii
2
3

Unit 06 Choices, Choices, Choices

Exercise 6.1

b bad for the environment
b can't be recycled easily
c more cultural understanding
a very special time for my family
a really delicious food
c better chance to learn languages
d created the turtle ship
c make great friends
b can be toxic
d inspired his soldiers
d won every battle
a many famous sites

Exercise 6.2

1. On Wednesday, Professor Baek gave a lecture on the Berlin Airlift.
2. Hello? I'm your neighbor. Can you please turn the volume down on the radio?
3. There was nothing good on television last night.
4. In my opinion, we should do more to stop global warning.
5. Christmas will fall on a Sunday this year.
6. Chapel class is a required coarse for freshmen.
7. You should go to bed early tonight.
8. Her name was written on the envelope.
9. The assignment is due on September eighteen.
10. We heard a weird noise outside the window.

Exercise 6.3

1. Please correct your mistakes.
2. There are some oranges in the kitchen if you want them.
3. Whose shoes are these?
4. The teacher called their parents.
5. You're coming with us tomorrow, right?
6. Now then, let's talk about tomorrow's test.
7. It's time to study, not play.

8. I don't know, maybe we should ask the professor whether this is right answer.
9. I hope the Bears don't lose the game tomorrow.
10. I am not sure where Hannah and Chulwon are; they're supposed be here now.
11. I don't think the weather will affect our plans very much.
12. This is your fault, not mine.
13. The dog was angry that the cat was drinking from its water bowl.
14. It's clear that we need a medical school at our university.
15. Sohee had more to drink than Kelly.
16. These pants are too loose; I need a smaller size.
17. The financial crisis had many effects.
18. Your sure they're going to help us move this weekend?
19. The Security Council did not know whether their actions would have any affect.
20. Rather than change their strategy, many banks continued buying mortgage securities.

Exercise 6.4

1. Really? Are you sure?
2. Oh my goodness!
3. Help! Call the police!
4. Can you do more to help save the environment?
5. There are two ways to solve this problem.

Exercise 6.5

1. Dayoung is a very diligent student.
2. Soongsil University was founded by Christian missionaries.
3. The cat sleeps all day.
4. An apple a day keeps the doctor away.
5. You are from Australia?
6. He goes to Japan tomorrow.
7. Tomorrow's class has been cancelled.
8. They were not happy about the new plan.
9. Minji and Wonho live in the dormitory, but Dahee lives at home.
10. What does the doctor need to know about my medical history?

Exercise 6.6

1. The exam is going to be / will be on Thursday.
2. Did you finish your homework before class?
3. When I was young, I studied in the Philippines.

4. She was eating when the phone rang.
5. Maria has been worken on her project for several weeks now.
6. This is my favorite movie.
7. When Hanbyeol saw the sunrise, he felt very lucky.
8. If you want to get a good score, you will need to prepare very diligently.
9. Polar bears have been endangered for a few decades now.
10. European exports have been declining for a long time but now are growing at a steady rate.

Exercise 6.7

1. Sally's birthday party is scheduled for Saturday, October 15th.
2. While Jesus Christ is the central figure for Protestants, Catholics and other Christians, many people don't know that he is considered a prophet in Islam and can even be found in some Hindu beliefs.
3. Well, that was interesting.
4. Frank asked if I knew what the homework was for Professor Smith's class.
5. I usually buy my groceries at Homeplus, or maybe Costco.
6. His favorite whiskey was Jameson, a famous Irish brand.
7. The child was reading Harry Potter and the Philosopher's Stone by J.K. Rowling.
8. Ban Ki Mun was the first Korean to be the Secretary General of the United Nations.
9. The U.S.S. Arizona was one of the many ships sunk by the Japanese in the attack on the U.S. naval base at Pearl Harbor, Hawai'i.
10. Last night we watched Inception on DVD.

Exercise 6.8

1. Well, I'm not sure.
2. Tiffany, Beth, and Seulgi went to the noraebang after the party.
3. The office is in Arlington, Virginia, USA.
4. Dr. Choi said, "You shouldnt drink any alcohol while you're taking this medicine."
5. We ordered the French quiche; it wasn't very good.
6. A large strange, red bump appeared on Jaeyoung's arm.
7. When I was in school, we would sometimes skip class to go fishing near Henry's farm.
8. Mercury pollution in the environment causes many problems: birth defects, mental problems, skin problems, and many other illnesses.
9. "That's mine!" the prince shouted at the thief but it was too late; he had escaped over the wall.
10. Late one night last summer, Mallory made an amazing, shocking, revolutionary discovery.

Unit 07 **Planning Makes Perfect**

Exercise 7.1

	Singular Pronoun	Possessive	Object	Plural Pronoun	Possessive	Object
1st	I	My	Me	We	Our	Us
2nd	You	Your	You	You	Your	You
3rd	*he*	*His*	*Him*	They	Their	Them
male	She	Her	Her			
female	It	Its	It			
neutral						

Exercise 7.2

1. If you are going to the store, can you buy some milk, please?
2. Sam's birthday is on Friday.
3. The first incident occurred in April.
4. The Statue of Liberty is one of the most famous landmarks in the USA.
5. You have until next Wednesday to finish the assignment.
6. They were reading *Les Misérables* by Victor Hugo.

Exercise 7.3

Seat Belts Save Lives

When people ride in a car, do they use the seatbelt? Everyone should always wear a seatbelt when they are in a car. There are several reasons for this opinion. First, seat belts save lives. A person has a one in five chance of getting into a car accident. According to statistics found on James Madison University's website, 35000 people die each year in the United States. What was shocking is that 50% of those people could have lived if they wore a seatbelt. Secondly, car accidents are responsible for most brain and spinal cord injuries. These kinds of injuries are easily avoidable if one wears a seatbelt. Finally, the website said that most children who die in a car accident are killed by an adult who is not wearing a seatbelt. So, it is clear, everyone must wear a seatbelt for themselves and for their family. When people buckle up, everyone wins!

Exercise 7.4

1. India has many interesting holidays like/such as the Festival of Diwali.
2. There have been many monster sightings around the world. For example/For instance, in Scotland, many people claim to have seen a dinosaur in Loch Ness.
3. Many delicious fruits grow in Malaysia like/such as rambutans, papaya, and starfruits.
4. Can you get some groceries, like butter and some vegetables for a salad, please?
5. Scientific discoveries can happen by accident. For example/for instance, penicillin was discovered when Alexander Fleming accidentally dropped some moldy bread into a petri dish of bacteria he was studying.

Exercise 7.5

1. gayageum
2. pork cutlet
3. kite
4. sushi
5. hanbok

Exercise 7.6

1. Do you want to go to Lotte World tomorrow?
2. There are several reasons for saving money.
3. I don't know; what do you want to do?
4. There has to be a better way to do this.
5. I think you should have gotten more sleep.

Exercise 7.7

big ········ large
get ········ have
see ········ observe
you ········ one
kind of ········ somewhat
stuff ········ items
kids ········ children
OK ········ acceptable
lot of ········ many/much

Unit 08 Putting It All Together

Exercise 8.1

1. University entrance exam
   (descriptive) Korea's university entrance exam plays an important role in students' lives.
   (persuasive) In my opinion, the university entrance exam is not a good way for universities to pick students
2. Learning English
   (descriptive) English language learning is increasing around the world
   (persuasive) English can only be learned through practice with native speakers.
3. China
   (descriptive) China has a long, rich history.
   (persuasive) China's growing influence in South Asia must be countered by other countries
4. Fashion trends
   (descriptive) What people consider fashionable every season are determined by designers in Paris and New York.
   (persuasive) Yves Saint Laurent was the most influential fashion designer of the 20th century.
5. Bill Gates
   (descriptive) Bill Gates has played an important role in the development of the personal computer.
   (persuasive) Bill Gates' charity work is more important than his development of Windows and Microsoft.

Exercise 8.2

I. Introduction
  A. How do you get around your city?
  B. "In my opinion, Seoul has a great public transportation system."
II. Body
  A. Cheap
    1. Bus costs
      i. Town bus = 800w
      ii. City bus = 1000w
    2. Subway costs
      i. 1000w/10km
    3. T-money card discount = 100w
  B. easy to use
    1. Use transport card
    2. Buy ticket
    3. Signs are clear and easy to read

C. convenient
   1. Many bus stops
   2. 9 subway lines and suburb lines
   3. Transfers between bus and subway = free
   4. iPhone apps, electronic signs

III. Conclusion
  A. Seoul's public transportation good, cheap, easy to use, convenient
  B. Try it!

Exercise 8.3

Reread your paragraph. Does it include all of the elements from the outline?

Unit 09 Reviewing the Basics

Exercise 9.1

1. An African bee flew into Becky's room.
2. The new store in COEX Mall had a sale on jeans.
3. On Wednesday Lieutenant Kim took the KTX to Busan.
4. Steven went to the PC room in Bongcheon to copy Jong-su's Japanese music DVD.
5. For her English class Won-hee has to read "One Hundred Years of Solitude."
6. The doctor from Chungang University Hospital was eating at Quizno's in Gangnam.
7. I just bought a Christian Dior dress for the Oscars ceremony in California next April.
8. Kim Yuna is one of the most famous Korean athletes, especially after the Beijing Olympics.
9. Finally, it is clear that we need to find a way to save Palau and the Maldives from sinking below the Pacific Ocean.
10. Gretchen was born in Switzerland but moved to Sydney, Australia when she was nine.

Exercise 9.2

1. Bee Season
2. Crime Scene Investigator
3. The Jewel in the Palace
4. The First Shop of The Coffee Prince
5. For Whom the Bell Tolls

6. A Brief History of Time
7. Hedwig and The Angry Inch
8. Zen and The Art of Motorcycle Maintenance
9. Super Mario Brothers
10. Pride and Prejudice

Exercise 9.3

In my opinion, we should always wear a seatbelt when we are in a car.
That's why I now only buy fair trade coffee.
While bears are important to Korea's culture, today they are in great danger.

Exercise 9.4

A Tragic Day

September 17th, 1862 was the single bloodiest day in United States history. On that day, near the town of Sharpsburg along Antietam Creek 23,000 men died fighting in the American Civil War. ~~On September 11th, 2001, only 3000 people died, so Antietam was worse.~~ The leader of the Southern Army, General Robert E. Lee had begun an invasion of the Northern States as part of the Maryland Campaign. The Northern leader, Major General George McClellan, had many more troops than Lee, but due to poor strategy failed to defeat the Southern army. In that day of the Battle of Antietam, more Americans were killed than in any other battle in the nation's history.

Exercise 9.5

For the Children

Granddaughter is six years old. She loves to play with her friends and draw pictures. But, she does not have much time to do these fun things because she goes to an English kindergarten at 9am every day. After she returns home at 3pm, she meets a Korean tutor for an hour, and then she goes with her brother to tae-kwon-do class. Why do our children have to study so much? When do they have time to be children? By the time they reach university, they are tired of studying. Our children cannot and should not endure so much stress. We MUST look at ways to change the education system so that children have a chance to be children.

Exercise 9.6

Some students were late.
The answer is wrong.
A mother and her baby were crossing the street.
Money and information are important in the global economy.
Tae-sub doesn't do his homework.
Alicia and Ji-yeon weren't at the meeting.
Tomorrow the weather is going to be awful.
If you drink too much soju, you will be sick tomorrow.
The new teacher wants to learn all the students' names.
There is a table and lamp in the bedroom.

Exercise 9.7

1. A butterfly landed on the flower.
2. The teacher gave a lot of homework.
3. Stephanie missed her bus.
4. Can you hand me the book, please?
5. If you are tired, drink some coffee.
6. Oh my god! It's a bee!
7. Do you know where the restaurant is?
8. Please help me!
9. We can do it if we try.
10. I don't know where the restaurant is.

Unit 10 Odds & Ends

Exercise 10.1

1. According to the news, it will snow tomorrow.
2. When we first came to school this building wasn't finished yet.
3. Because I was late, I missed the quiz.
4. Sarah didn't know who was knocking on the door.
5. Families are hurting because of the economic recession.
6. Since the price increased last month, people are buying fewer heads of cabbage.
7. Meet me where the bus stops.
8. Anyone who lives in Gyeonggi-do should be able to live in the dorm.
9. Listening to her iPod, Claire didn't hear the phone ring.
10. In my opinion taxes are too high.

Exercise 10.2

Some words may fit in different boxes.

Continuing a Thought	Contrast
and, additionally, moreover, furthermore, following this further, also, in addition, in the same way	on the contrary, however, yet, but, on the other hand, nevertheless
Opening	**Continuing**
in the first place, in the light of the... it is	finally, therefore, in final consideration, in conclusion, hence, in final analysis
Confirmation	**General Use**
clearly then, obviously, certainly ,of course, undoubtedly, to be sure, indeed	admittedly, unquestionably, because, easy to see that, besides that, consequently, no doubt

Exercise 10.3

1. will go
2. resigned
3. sleeps
4. drink
5. runs
6. met
7. will be
8. is
9. said / will come
10. didn't study / will get

Exercise 10.4

1. am going to see
2. were talking
3. are starting / are going to start
4. are adding
5. are going to wait
6. is going to make

Exercise 10.5

1. have made
2. has studied

3. will have spent
4. had seen (has seen)
5. will have used

Exercise 10.6

Introduction

The other day my family and I wanted to visit my wife's family farm in Gangwondo. We jumped in the car and started our drive. Eight hours later, we finally arrived, exhausted and annoyed. It was non-stop traffic all the way there! Driving in and around Seoul is even worse. Going to work by car is almost impossible, so usually I take the subway, even though the station is far from my house and my job. I believe it is time for the government to begin taxing cars heavily. There are three reasons for this proposal: taxes will discourage people from purchasing cars, it will raise income for the government to spend on roads and transportation, and it encourages people to use public transportation.

body

If something costs a lot, most people can't buy it. That is a simple fact. Right now, cars are too cheap, so almost anyone can buy a car if they want it. Many families in Seoul have two cars now. However, there is no room on Seoul's streets for these cars. Unless there is a heavy tax on cars, people will keep buying too many. Of course, this will be difficult for poor families that might need a car for work, so the government could make a tax that affects rich people more than poor people. Further, the government will have to give some benefit to car makers like Hyundai and Kia; perhaps a tax break for them, or some other consideration would make it more acceptable.

Money from taxes helps the government provide for the people of the nation. With more taxes from cars, the government can improve the road and highway system. Larger and better highways between Seoul and the provinces would be especially useful. Bus lanes could be added to even more streets to improve the public transportation system. Or perhaps the tax money could be used to expand the KTX system, with new lines to Seocho and other cities that are currently difficult to reach. As long as the new tax money is used wisely to help the traffic and transportation system, then the people will feel a great benefit from the tax.

Finally, a tax as I've proposed will encourage people to use subways, trains and buses, because if fewer people buy cars, more people will need to use public transportation. There are many benefits from this. First, it will reduce traffic on the streets, of course. Second, it will preserve the environment, since public transportation is much more energy efficient than cars. Third, it makes the transportations more profitable and allows them to improve and expand their services. As we all know, the subway system especially needs to remodel many of their stations; so if they have more customers, they will have more money to fix their problems.

Conclusion

Therefore, for these three reasons, I want the government to propose a new tax on car sales. Such a tax will improve traffic conditions, raise money for road and transportation systems, and encourage use of buses and subways which have many advantages. Please help me to support this proposal by emailing, calling, or writing letters to members of the National Assembly. Send letters to the local newspapers. Post this message to your blog or homepage. If we work together, we can improve our country!

Exercise 10.8

1. What is the essay's hook?
   Personal story about driving to Gangwondo
2. What is the essay's thesis statement?
   "I believe it is time for the government to begin taxing cars heavily."
3. What are the three main points to support the thesis?
   taxes will discourage people from purchasing cars
   it will raise income for the government to spend on roads and transportation
   it encourages people to use public transportation
4. What is the essay's challenge?
   "Please help me to support this proposal by emailing, calling, or writing letters to members of the National Assembly. Send letters to the local newspapers. Post this message to your blog or homepage."
5. What is the essay's memento or closing statement?
   "If we work together, we can improve our country!"
6. Find ten signal words in the essay.

however	of course	further	finally	or perhaps
as long as	first	second	third	therefore

Unit 11 Ideas & Organization

Exercise 11.1

1. colder
2. spicier
3. harder
4. higher
5. better
6. more diligently / worse
7. more interesting
8. more expensive
9. lazier
10. sadder

Exercise 11.2

1. the funniest
2. the most beautiful
3. the lowest
4. the most delicious
5. the best
6. most deadly
7. the most disgusting
8. the best / the worst
9. the most difficult
10. the runniest

Exercise 11.3

These are suggested answers. Your answers may be different.

1. The Eiffel Tower is more famous than the Louvre.
2. Taking the KTX is usually cheaper than flying.
3. I like Ferrari better than Porsche.
4. She prefers Gucci over Armani.
5. Love is stronger than hate.
6. I think Girls' Generation is more entertaining than the Wonder Girls.
7. China is growing faster than the USA.
8. I usually go to Starbucks more often than Angel-in-us.
9. Pepero Day is sillier than White Day.
10. You are funnier than your best friend.

Exercise 11.4

1. strongest last
2. chronological
3. problem/solution
4. cause/effect

Unit 12 Begin at the Beginning

Exercise 12.1

Mark the hook, the thesis statement and the preview in these introductions.

1. What's your earliest memory? For me, it was walking through a grassy field in a park on a bright spring day. I was three and I got stung by a bee on my arm. Most importantly, according to my mom, it never happened. Memory is a mysterious, amazing thing. In this essay, I will explain how the brain forms memories, how memory changes over time, and how false memories occur.

2. When the Church forced the astronomer Galileo Galilee to say that the Earth does not revolve around the sun, he sent secret letters to other scholars telling them about his discoveries. Galileo was just one of many scientists whose voice had been silenced by religious and political organizations. There are many reasons why this happens. Religious leaders worry that discoveries will challenge people's faith. Political leaders fear losing power. Finally, people generally dislike change.

3. "Shaken, not stirred." If you've ever seen a James Bond movie, you've heard this famous line as the international spy orders a martini. Martinis are a classy drink and anyone can look sophisticated ordering one. In this essay, I'll tell you about the martini's history, the different kinds of martinis, and how to make your own at home.

Exercise 12.2

1. C
2. B
3. A
4. C
5. A

Exercise 12.3

1. C
2. D
3. A
4. F
5. E
6. B

Unit 13 Supporting the Thesis

Exercise 13.1

Transportation	Historical sites	Dining	Shopping	Culture
subway taxis buses KTX	Gyeongbokgung Changdeokgung Namdaemun Deoksugung	fire chicken Korean BBQ rice porridge ddeokboki kimchi	Namdaemun market COEX Myeongdong Dongdaemun market Ewha fashion district	Seou Art Center Leeum Samsung Museum Gahoe Museum Sejong Art Center

Exercise 13.2

1. In my opinion, the government and industry must reduce carbon emissions.
   ~~A. Carbon can form diamonds under extreme pressure over long periods of time.~~
2. Before you can love someone else in a lasting and healthy way, you have to love yourself.
   ~~A. Scientists have discovered that there are several chemicals in the brain related to love.~~
3. There are several things you should watch for when buying a notebook computer.
   ~~A. HP merged with Compaq several years ago, making the new company one of the largest tech companies in the world.~~

Unit 14 Ending on a High Note

Exercise 14.1

1. C
2. A
3. B

Exercise 14.2

1. If you're drinking this weekend, be sure to have some seaweed soup the next morning.
2. Please, share this message with your friends and save the poor animals.
3. Next time you buy a cell phone, get a smartphone.

Exercise 14.3

1. You'll be happy you did.
2. It's the right thing to do.
3. You'll be connected to everyone, all the time, everywhere. Welcome to the future!

Unit 15 Are You Ready to Write?

Exercise 15.1

I. Introduction
  1. (hook) ask reader if they have a pet, what kind do they like
  2. (thesis) I think dogs are the best kind of pet.
  3. (preview)
     A. dogs more fun
     B. dogs smarter
     C. dogs more loving

II. Body
  1. Dogs more fun
     A. run and chase
     B. bring things back to you
     C. Cats chase mice; dogs more exciting
  2. Dogs smarter
     A. Animal trainers: dogs easier to train
     B. dogs can remember more commands
     C. cats can learn, but dogs easier to teach
  3. Dogs more loving
     A. wolves live in packs
     B. Cats = loners, can live alone
     C. when you come home, dogs are excited

III. Conclusion

1. (summary) dogs are better pets because they are smart, fun, and loving
2. cats okay, dogs better________________
3. (memento) get a dog

Exercise 15.2

1. Many students work part-time jobs.
2. These days, our nation has several problems.
3. She collects dolls and old books.
4. In fall, I love to eat mandarin oranges from Jeju Island.
5. If I had a lot of money, I'd buy a few things for my family.

Exercise 15.3

1. should
2. would
3. would
4. could
5. should

Unit 16 Putting It All Together

Exercise 16.1

I. Introduction

A. (hook) 380,000 die from e.coli

B. (topic sentence) we can reduce e.coli deaths if we know about it

II. Body

A. (detail 1) e.coli is spread by unclean food

B. (detail 2) spread is preventable by education, good farm supplies, water facilities

C. (detail 3) organizations are fighting e.coli

III. Conclusion

A. (challenge) please donate time and money

B. (memenot) efforts will save lives

Exercise 16.2

When you look at the night sky, do you wonder if there is anyone up there? Since ancient times, people have looked to the sky for answers to that question. The scientists at SETI are very concerned with that question. In this essay we will look at who SETI is, how they look for alien life, and learn about their most intriguing discovery.

First, SETI stands for the Search for Extra-Terrestrial Intelligence. SETI is not one specific group of people, however. There are many activities around the world through various universities and private research facilities that contribute to the search for aliens. While some experiments were performed as early as 1896, SETI as we know it today began in 1960 at Cornell University by astronomer Frank Drake. Today, thousands of astronomers, hobbyists, and others spend at least part of their time looking for alien life.

Secondly, let us look at how SETI works. Using giant telescopes around the world, they search through the vast amount of space looking for signs from intelligent civilizations on distant planets. Various projects at large telescopes and universities around the world use radio signals and other data to look for signs of intelligent civilizations on other planets. In the early years, getting enough equipment to search for these signs was a problem. By contrast, today there is too much data to examine easily, so an innovative computer program called SETI@home was developed. Anyone can download this software which uses their computer whenever it's not busy. Through this method, billions of mathematical calculations can be performed with little effort.

Finally, has SETI found any proof of alien life? Actually, thus far, no definite proof of life on another planets have been found. In 1977, though, a mysterious radio signal was discovered by a SETI researcher in Ohio. The signal seemed like it might be from an intelligent civilization. The researcher was so surprised, he wrote "Wow!" on the printout. Unfortunately the Wow signal was never repeated, so scientists could not confirm it.

As you can see, SETI is an interesting set of projects and study that looks for signs of intelligent life on other worlds. While no proof of aliens has been seen yet, their efforts have helped to innovate many technologies for space exploration. Maybe someday we will find another Wow signal from someone, somewhere in the universe.

Memo

Christopher R. Sanders

EDUCATIONAL HISTORY

- 2002 Master, Computer Information Systems
  University of Phoenix Tulsa, Oklahoma
- 1999 Bachelor, Political Science
  University of Tulsa, Oklahoma

PROFESSIONAL HISTORY

- 2007 ~ Present 숭실대학교 베어드학부대학 교수
- 2004 ~ 2007 SLP Program Coordinator
- 2002 ~ 2004 Vatterot College, Tulsa, Oklahoma 교수

Foundation of Freshman English Writing

초판발행	2011년 3월 3일
2쇄발행	2013년 7월 19일
지 은 이	Christopher R. Sanders
펴 낸 이	한 헌 수
펴 낸 곳	숭실대학교 출판국 서울 동작구 상도로 369
등 록	제14-2호(1982. 1. 25) TEL 02-820-0771~2 FAX 02-817-5297 http://press.ssu.ac.kr
찍 은 곳	한컴인쇄정보 TEL 02-2274-3394 FAX 02-2274-3397

값 13,000원

ISBN 978-89-7450-266-9 03740